What Drives China's Economy

The spectacular economic growth experienced by China since 1978 has often been hailed as the "China Miracle". Many economists have tried to understand the forces behind China's phenomenal growth and the explanations can be divided into two broad schools of economic thought – one school of thought which includes Nobel Laureate Paul Krugman explains that market mechanism and deregulation led to China's success, while the other school of thought which includes Justin Yifu Lin, the former Chief Economist and Senior Vice-President of the World Bank, explains that China's growth miracle is a unique model to itself defined by the Chinese government's prominent role. The Chinese government has been responsible in identifying and investing in industries that have contributed to economic growth. Some economists in the latter school even claim that the China Miracle cannot be explained by mainstream economics.

This book examines both schools of thought and attempts to provide a synthesis of the two schools to explain the China Miracle. It looks at the Solow-Swan growth model, the Harrod-Domar model and transaction cost theory. It provides insights into whether and how China can sustain its growth and how developing countries may replicate China's success.

Qing-Ping Ma currently works at Nottingham University Business School China. He has published two books on economics, *Private Capital and Road to Developed Economy* (editor) and *The Theory and Practice of Pensions and Social Security*, and articles on pension economics and China's economic growth.

Routledge Focus on Economics and Finance

The fields of economics are constantly expanding and evolving. This growth presents challenges for readers trying to keep up with the latest important insights. Routledge Focus on Economics and Finance presents short books on the latest big topics, linking in with the most cutting-edge economics research.

Individually, each title in the series provides coverage of a key academic topic, whilst collectively the series forms a comprehensive collection across the whole spectrum of economics.

Microfinance
Research, Debates, Policy
Bernd Balkenhol

The Malaysian Banking Industry
Policies and Practices after the Asian Financial Crisis
Rozaimah Zainudin, Chan Sok Gee and Aidil Rizal Shahrin

Automation, Capitalism and the End of The Middle Class
Jon-Arild Johannessen

Cryptocurrencies
A Primer on Digital Money
Mark Grabowski

Knowledge Infrastructure and Higher Education in India
Kaushalesh Lal and Shampa Paul

What Drives China's Economy
Economic, Socio-Political, Historical and Cultural Factors
Qing-Ping Ma

For a full list of titles in this series, please visit www.routledge.com/series/RFEF

What Drives China's Economy

Economy

Economic, Socio-Political,
Historical and Cultural Factors

Qing-Ping Ma

Routledge
Taylor & Francis Group

LONDON AND NEW YORK

First published 2020
by Routledge
2 Park Square, Milton Park, Abingdon, Oxon OX14 4RN

and by Routledge
52 Vanderbilt Avenue, New York, NY 10017

Routledge is an imprint of the Taylor & Francis Group, an informa business

British Library Cataloguing-in-Publication Data
A catalogue record for this book is available from the British Library

Library of Congress Cataloging-in-Publication Data
Names: Ma, Qing-Ping, author.
Title: What drives China's economy : economic, socio-political,
    historical and cultural factors / Qing-Ping Ma.
Description: New York : Routledge, 2020. | Series: Routledge focus
    on economics and finance | Includes bibliographical references
    and index.
Identifiers: LCCN 2019042530 (print) | LCCN 2019042531 (ebook)
Subjects: LCSH: China—Economic policy—21st century. | Monetary
    policy—China. | Investments—China. | Economic development—
    Government policy—China.
Classification: LCC HC427.95 .M3343 2020 (print) |
    LCC HC427.95 (ebook) | DDC 330.951—dc23
LC record available at https://lccn.loc.gov/2019042530
LC ebook record available at https://lccn.loc.gov/2019042531

ISBN: 978-0-367-17975-5 (hbk)
ISBN: 978-0-429-05878-3 (ebk)

Typeset in Times New Roman
by Apex CoVantage, LLC

To my parents, Ma Yao and Li Pei-Lan, with gratitude

Contents

Figures

Preface

China's rapid economic growth since 1978 has attracted great interest from both policy-makers and scholars. Many economists have conducted researches to understand the causes of this "China Miracle". Their ideas can be classified into two schools of thought. One school thinks that introducing market mechanism and deregulation can explain China's fast growth, while the other school believes that China has found a new growth model, the China Model or Beijing Consensus, with an active role for government in identifying and actively supporting industries that contribute to economic growth. Some economists in the second school claim that the China Miracle cannot be explained by the mainstream economics. Although many books and articles have been written on China's reform and opening as well as its phenomenal growth, this book tries to give a more broad-based analysis on the causes of the China Miracle and the future of China's economic growth.

The plan to write a broad-based analysis on China's rapid growth arose from my perception of discrepancy between the popular narratives of China's reform and the history I have witnessed. I spent the first 30 years of my life in China, living through the Cultural Revolution, the period when Hua Guofeng was China's Wise Leader, the first ten years of China's reform and opening with the failure of "crossing the price pass" in 1988, the rectification and consolidation during 1989–1991 and the re-ignition of the growth engine by Deng Xiaoping's southern trip in 1992. My personal experience of China's reform and opening might have helped me understand the economic, social, cultural and historical factors that underlie China's rapid economic growth better than scholars who have not lived in China during that period. Empirical studies on China's economic growth have identified many contributing factors such as capital input, total productivity factor (TPF), foreign direct investment (FDI), education, improved health and demographic dividends, but these factors are probably secondary to the socio-political conditions in the post–Mao Zedong China and the enterprising spirit of ordinary Chinese people. This book analyzes the factors that underlie China's rapid growth through examining the history of its reform and opening as well as its socio-political conditions.

Popular narratives often overstate the roles of some historical figures and credit them with achievements that cannot be justified by historical facts, and diminish the contribution of some other figures. The truth of events in the history of reform and opening is important to understanding what factors underlie China's rapid growth and whether there is a unique China Model for economic growth that contradicts the Washington Consensus. Therefore, Chapter 1 of this book briefly reviews the history of importing Western equipment and technology in the early 1970s as well as China's reform and opening. A key finding from this review of history is that the enterprising spirit of ordinary Chinese people and grassroots initiatives are the real driving force of China's rapid economic growth, while the role of China's leadership was mainly to become less and less inhibitive to the grassroots initiatives. Hua Guofeng, Deng Xiaoping, Hu Yaobang, Zhao Ziyang and many others have made important contribution in making the Communist Party of China more tolerant to the entrepreneurship and business innovations of Chinese people.

To address the issue whether China's success can be explained by the mainstream economics, Chapter 2 presents a growth through interest rate control model in which high national saving rates and high investment rates drive China's rapid growth since 1978. This chapter shows that the true miracle is how China has maintained its high saving rates for over four decades rather than China's high growth rates. Chapter 3 analyzes why market economies under authoritarian regimes and centrally planned economies might grow faster than market economies in democracies for a fairly long period, by examining the Ramsey model and the market economy solution to the Ramsey's problem by Cass and Koopmans. This chapter shows that the political, historical and cultural factors in China have reduced transaction costs, increased transaction efficiency, supported high saving rates and high investment rates and maintained social stability, which underlie China's rapid growth since 1978. Chapter 4 discusses whether China's success can be replicated by other developing countries, whether China can maintain its rapid growth and what China should do to realize its growth potential in the future.

China's economic growth following its reform and opening is a success story among the previous centrally planned economies in their transition to market economy as well as among the developing countries in their efforts to reduce poverty and to industrialize. Elucidating the causes and outcomes of different paths chosen by China, Russia, other republics of the former

Soviet Union and East European countries will deepen our understanding of economics especially development economics. I hope that readers will find this book helpful in understanding China's rapid economic growth in particular and economic development issues in general.

Qing-Ping Ma

Acknowledgements

I would like to express special thanks to Yongling Lam, editor at Taylor & Francis Asia Pacific for her encouragement in writing this book. I also thank Samantha Phua and Felicia Hor at Taylor & Francis Asia Pacific for their help.

Abbreviations

ABC	Agricultural Bank of China
BOC	Bank of China
CBTE	commune, production brigade or team-run enterprise
CCB	China Construction Bank
CHIBOR	China Interbank Offered Rate
CNY	Chinese yuan
CPC	Communist Party of China
FDI	foreign direct investment
GDP	gross domestic product
GNI	gross national income
ICBC	Industrial and Commercial Bank of China
IPO	initial public offering
LIBOR	London Interbank Offered Rate
MPK	marginal product of capital
MPL	marginal product of labour
MPS	Material Product System
OECD	Organisation of Economic Cooperation and Development
PBOC	People's Bank of China
PPP	purchasing power parity
PRC	People's Republic of China
RMB	Renminbi
RPI	retail price index
SHIBOR	Shanghai Interbank Offered Rate
SNA	System of National Accounting
SOE	state-owned enterprise
SOU	state-owned units
SWF	social welfare function
TVE	township and village enterprise
UCOE	urban collectively owned enterprise
UK	United Kingdom
US	United States
VPN	virtual private network

1 A brief history of China's reform and opening

China's rapid economic growth since 1978 has often been hailed as the "China Miracle" (Lin, Cai, and Li 2003). From 1978 to 2018, China's real gross domestic product (GDP) grew at an average annual rate of around 9.5%. Its economy has grown more than 40-fold in real terms and its real per capita GDP more than 18-fold. Since the Chinese experience appears to be inconsistent with the conventional wisdom or the Washington Consensus that emphasizes the importance of property rights and free markets in maintaining long-term economic growth (Williamson 2000), many economists think that China has found a new road to economic prosperity, the China Model or Beijing Consensus, for developing countries (Ramo 2004; Zhang 2006). Some of them think that modern economics cannot explain China's phenomenal growth and there is a need to develop new economic theories (Hu 2008; Lin 2008). Many mainstream development economists who are free market supporters disagree with the concept of a China Model. To them, the increasing role of the market has served as the foundation of China's rapid growth (Summers and Thomas 1993; Huang 2008; Williamson 2012).

Scholars advocating the China Model generally acknowledge the importance of introducing market mechanism in the China Miracle (Lin 2013). They also agree that many other factors that are important according to modern development economics have contributed to China's rapid growth. One such factor is the advantage of backwardness in China's pursuit of technological innovation and structural transformation (Lin 2013), which enables it to "catch up" with developed countries by acquiring advanced technologies from them (Gerschenkron 1962; Abramovitz 1986). Several studies also find that foreign direct investment (FDI) improves firm productivity and contributes positively to China's economic growth (Zhang and Felmingham 2002; Chuang and Hsu 2004; Hu, Jefferson, and Jinchang 2005; Jefferson and Su 2006; Van Reenen and Yueh 2012). Some advocates of the China Model, however, believe that something special underlies China's success. Their main argument lies in that many countries with more market mechanism and less government control than China have worse performance in economic growth.

Although mainstream economists may disagree with the claim that modern economics cannot explain China's rapid growth, many of them do find that China has been somehow different (Murphy, Shleifer, and Vishny 1992). Nolan and Wang think that China's large state-owned enterprises (SOEs) do not fit neatly into existing patterns, which presents a challenge to the "transitional orthodoxy" and to ideas concerning property rights in development economics (Nolan and Wang 1999). Alberto Gabriele shows that the role of the state in China is massive, dominant and crucial to China's industrial development (Gabriele 2010). Gregory C. Chow thinks that China's rapid economic growth poses several challenges to economics on topics such as private versus public ownership, modern legal system versus "guanxi" (the Chinese term for close social connections), individual versus collective welfare and multiparty versus one-party systems (Chow 1997).

To understand what underlies China's rapid growth over the past four decades, whether China has found a growth model for developing countries and whether modern economics can explain China's rapid growth, the best starting point would be to examine what has happened in the past four decades. This chapter will briefly review the history of China's reform and opening and reflect on the arguments of different economists in their interpretation of China's rapid economic growth. Since epoch-making events rarely occur without a prelude, it will be helpful to include in this chapter China's efforts to improve the living standard of its people in the eve of the reform and opening and the final years of Mao Zedong as the Chairman of the Central Committee of the Communist Party of China (CPC).

1.1   Western technology import and commune-run enterprises before October 1976

The current narratives of China's reform and opening often give an impression that China was entirely closed to the outside world before the Third Plenum of the Eleventh Central Committee of the CPC held during 18–22 December 1978. Introduction of advanced foreign technologies by importing complete sets of equipment from Western countries actually started well before 1978. Even during the Cultural Revolution (1966–1976) China did not completely close its door. After the early upheaval of the Cultural Revolution, several events in the early 1970s created new opportunities for China to connect with the outside world. These included ping-pong diplomacy between China and the United States (US) in 1971, the replacement of Taiwan by the mainland as China's sole legal representative in the United Nations on 25 October 1971 and the visit to China by the US President

Richard Nixon during 21–28 February 1972. The downfall of Lin Biao[1] and his followers during 1970–1971 strengthened the influence of Zhou Enlai, Premier of the State Council (the central government), who was generally considered a pragmatist and keen for China's economic construction.

Under instructions from Mao Zedong and Zhou Enlai, the *Report on Importing Complete Sets of Chemical Fibres and Chemical Fertilizers Producing Equipment* was drafted by Chen Jinhua,[2] signed by Li Xiannian,[3] Hua Guofeng[4] and Yu Qiuli,[5] and submitted to Zhou Enlai. Zhou Enlai and Mao Zedong approved it on 5 and 7 February 1972 respectively. The report proposed to import four complete sets of chemical fibre–producing equipment with capacity of 240,000 tons, two complete sets of 300,000-ton synthetic ammonia–producing equipment, and key equipment, spare parts and steel for construction or renovation of other chemical fertilizer factories, with a budget of US$400 million (Chen 2005). The Ministry of Light Industry and the Ministry of Fuel and Chemical Industries were responsible for implementing the plan. Delegations were sent to Western Europe and Japan to study potential suppliers, and the search for appropriate sites for those plants was also under way.

Li Xiannian and Yu Qiuli told Chen Jinhua a story which might have contributed to the decision by Mao Zedong and Zhou Enlai. On an inspection tour by Mao Zedong in southern China in 1971, one of his service staff came back late one day and told him that she queued for hours in order to buy some Dacron fabric which was in short supply. Later Mao asked Zhou Enlai why China had not produced more Dacron, and Zhou told him that China did not have the technology to produce polyesters. Mao then asked whether China could buy it from abroad; Zhou said that we could buy it from Western countries. After that conversation, Zhou Enlai instructed the State Council Working Group and the State Planning Commission to prepare a report on importing chemical fibre–producing equipment and chemical fertilizer–producing equipment. At the time, meeting people's basic need for food and clothes was still a serious challenge for the CPC leadership.

These projects encouraged other ministries to submit their plans to import advanced foreign equipment in their fields and to send delegations abroad to investigate advanced technologies for importing. The Ministry of Metallurgical Industry proposed to import 1.7-metre steel plate cool rolling equipment and accessories for Wuhan Iron and Steel at a cost of US$200 million, and the plan was approved on 21 August 1972 by the CPC Central Committee and the State Council. More projects were proposed afterwards. Under the instruction of Zhou Enlai, those project proposals were lumped together to form the *Request for Instruction on Increasing Equipment Import and Expanding Economic Exchange* submitted by the State Planning Commission to the State Council and Premier Zhou on 2 January 1973. It proposed to import complete sets of equipment worth US$4.3 billion over the next three to five years, hence it was called the 43 Plan. Total investment costs were about 21.4 billion Chinese yuan (CNY, also represented by RMB, standing for the Chinese currency Renminbi, i.e. people's money), which was a large-scale import program, as China's total capital construction investment in 1972 was CNY 41.2 billion. This was the second wave of importing foreign equipment and technologies. The first wave was the 156 projects assisted by the Soviet Union in the 1950s, which helped China build a relatively complete industrial system and start its transition from an agricultural economy with sparse industry to an industrial economy (Chen 1999; Tang 2004; Li, Peng, and Huang 2006).

The 43 Plan included 26 projects, including a petrochemical complex for producing chemical fibres (240,000 tons) and chemicals, chemical fertilizer plants (with capacity to produce 4 million tons of ammonia and 6.3 million tons of urea), power stations and steel rolling plants, which were completed between 1976 and 1982, just in time for the CPC to shift its focus to economic development and to improving the living conditions of the Chinese people. The actual expenditure was US$3.96 billion. Production of chemical fibres, fertilizers and electricity by those plants and factories played a key role in meeting the domestic demand for clothes, food and electricity in the early 1980s (Chen 2005). Without those plants and factories constructed before 1978, the reform and opening policy would not have achieved its perceived success in satisfying the demand for food, clothes and electricity. Many coastal rural areas started to have access to electricity in 1970 and cities were still often plagued by power cuts in the 1970s.

Mechanization of agriculture has been considered the key to meet people's need for food. A Chinese Agricultural Delegation led by Xiang Nan[6] visited the US during August and September 1976 to investigate American agricultural mechanization; the delegation was proposed by Hua Guofeng, then Premier of the State Council and First Vice-Chairman of the CPC, and approved by Mao Zedong (Chinese Society of Agricultural Machinery 1978; Xiang 1979; Gong 2016). Xiang Nan reported their findings to Hua Guofeng who was Chairman of the CPC and Premier of the State Council at the beginning of 1977, showed him the documentary films taken by the delegation and proposed to learn from the advanced experience of capitalist countries for realizing China's Four Modernizations.[7] Hua Guofeng was surprised by the prosperity of the US and its advanced level of agricultural mechanization (Han 2011), which might be one factor why Hua later became a strong supporter of importing advanced foreign equipment and technologies.

Mao Zedong had enthusiastically promoted the development of commune-run (industrial and commercial) enterprises and called them "our great bright hope" in 1959 (Feng 2007). Although the CPC Central Committee no longer encouraged people's communes to set up new industrial enterprises following the failure of the Great Leap Forward and the famine in the early 1960s, many communes, production brigades and production teams[8] continued to set up and run industrial enterprises, especially during the Cultural Revolution. In his famous 7 May Instruction,[9] Mao Zedong called on farmers to set up factories collectively. The commune, production brigade and team-run enterprises (CBTEs) usually arose from grassroots initiatives without central planning and provided services to local communities such as flour mills, oil mills, tofu workshops, noodle workshops, tailor shops, home appliance repair shops, local specialty factories and agricultural machinery repair factories. Some CBTEs processed parts for SOEs and urban collectively owned enterprises (UCOEs).

Under Mao Zedong's instruction on 27 September 1975, Deng Xiaoping[10] arranged two letters and one investigation report on CBTEs issued as a document of the Symposium on Rural Work of the CPC Central Committee. One letter to Chairman Mao and the CPC Central Committee was written on 5 September 1975 by Zhou Changgeng on behalf of some fellow staff members of Yongkang County People's Bank in Zhejiang Province, and they requested clear policies on the development of CBTEs. To support their case, they attached a letter written by Hua Guofeng on 28 December 1974 to the CPC Hunan Provincial Committee on promoting CBTE growth and an investigation report on CBTE development in Huiguozhen Commune of Gong County in Henan Province, "The Bright Hope" published by *Henan Daily* on 15 December 1974. The organ of the CPC Central Committee, *People's Daily*, reprinted the report under the title "The Great Bright Hope" on 11 October 1975, with a commentary "Enthusiastically Running Well Commune, Brigade and Team Enterprises". These activities gave new impetus to CBTE growth. By the end of 1976, there were 1.115 million CBTEs whose industrial output reached CNY 24.35 billion, which was 3.8% of the national industrial output (Wang 2017). These CBTEs accumulated capital, provided opportunities for entrepreneurs and trained talents, which laid the foundation for the flourishing township and village enterprises (TVEs) in the 1980s and 1990s.

The growth of CBTEs and later TVEs was driven by the inherent enterprising spirit of the Chinese people. The hardship for ordinary Chinese people over thousands of years to make a living and the Confucian teaching for self-reliance have instilled in them a strong enterprising spirit, which is well demonstrated by the large number of successful businesspeople of Chinese origin around the world. There are also many highly talented administrators and managers within the CPC who are willing to work hard in order that the Chinese people can live a happy life. China's economic development and standard of living were far below those achieved by the Soviet Union and East European countries, which made it possible to grow rapidly even under a similar central planning system. However, although Mao Zedong wanted to improve the life of ordinary people, his constant worry about capitalist restoration by private entrepreneurs and his de-facto monopoly of decision-making power hindered the full utilization of the talent and experiences of both other leaders and ordinary citizens. The communist spirit which he preached until his death failed to provide adequate incentives to managers, workers and farmers. The many political campaigns, which he launched to consolidate the proletarian dictatorship and to prevent capitalist restoration by rooting out bourgeois ideology and capitalist roaders, consumed people's energy and time which could be used for economic construction.

1.2   The death of Mao Zedong and the transition period from 1976 to 1978

Although China's reform and opening are usually considered to begin in 1978, the death of Mao Zedong on 9 September 1976 and the arrest of his widow Jiang Qing[11] and her three senior supporters (the Gang of Four)[12] who were Mao's protégés on 6 October 1976 marks a turning point in the modern history of China. Hua Guofeng who masterminded the arrest of the Gang of Four became Chairman of the CPC Central Committee and Chairman of the CPC Central Military Committee on 7 October 1976, with support from most veteran revolutionaries, many of whom had been humiliated or sidelined during the Cultural Revolution. Some senior officials who rose to high positions during the Cultural Revolution also supported Hua Guofeng. This change made it possible for China to pursue a different path of economic growth from that set by Mao. Six months earlier, the unofficial commemoration of Zhou Enlai around 5 April 1976 in Beijing and many other cities[13] (which was put down by the government as a counterrevolutionary activity and later called the 5 April Movement) had already shown that the Gang of Four and Mao's policies were disliked by the masses. The Gang of Four was accused mainly of two crimes: 1) carrying out fascist dictatorship and persecuting veteran CPC cadres as well as ordinary people and 2) sabotaging socialist economic construction, which caused China's economy to slide to the brink of collapse and fail to meet people's basic food and clothing needs. The accusations resonated well with public mood and won the new CPC leadership great public support. They also obliged the leadership to rehabilitate veteran cadres purged during the Cultural Revolution and to make economic development one of their top priorities.

In order to be viewed as Mao Zedong's legitimate political heir, Hua Guofeng and his supporters decorated their actions as following Mao's thought and instructions. The publication of *On the Ten Major Relationships*, an internal speech by Mao Zedong in 1956, on 26 December 1976 foretold many policies that would be implemented in the following years. The leadership under Hua Guofeng reaffirmed the objective of realizing Four Modernizations by the end of the 20th century espoused by Zhou Enlai in 1975. Deng Xiaoping was restored to his previous positions in July 1977. Because of his emphasis on economic performance, he was purged in early 1976 for the second time in ten years by Mao Zedong. The leadership set forth a series of new policies under the slogan "Grasp the Key Link and Stabilize the Country" to promote political stability and economic recovery, which was confirmed as a strategic decision by the Eleventh National Congress of the CPC held during 12–18 August 1977 (Central Committee of the Communist Party of China 1977).

Introduction of advanced foreign technologies and equipment and expansion of international trade, especially exports, as key approaches for modernization were policies made during this period. By the 1970s, the outcome of peaceful competition between the socialist camp and the capitalist camp advocated by the former Soviet leader Nikita Khrushchev became clear in terms of ordinary people's living standards. China's leaders were aware of the capitalist success and eager to learn from Western countries. However, they still strongly believed in the fundamental superiority of the socialist system; to them, what needed to be learned from the West were advanced technologies and management experiences. In July 1977, the State Planning Commission proposed to import additionally US$6.5 billion worth of complete sets of production equipment, single machines and patented technologies, in addition to finishing the 43 Plan projects and putting them into operation early. The Politburo of the CPC Central Committee approved the proposal in principle, and Deng Xiaoping thought there should be more, for example US$10 billion. The State Planning Commission later submitted a plan for importing US$15 billion worth of equipment and technologies, which was endorsed by Deng Xiaoping (Han 2011). Many delegations were sent to developed countries by various ministries and commissions under the State Council in the second half of 1977, including the economic delegation led by Yuan Baohua[14] to visit the United Kingdom (UK) and France. The future Baoshan Steel Works was discussed and planned in 1977 (Zhu 1995; Chen 2005).

At the Fifth National People's Congress (the legislature) of the People's Republic of China (PRC) during 26 February–5 March 1978, Hua Guofeng presented the draft of an ambitious ten-year plan for the 1976–1985 period. The plan called for high rates of growth in both industry and agriculture, and included 120 construction projects that would require massive and expensive imports of foreign technologies. More delegations were sent abroad in 1978 to investigate the advanced economies, including four delegations sent by the central government, the Economic Delegation led by Lin Hujia[15] to Japan from 28 March to 22 April 1978, the CPC Delegation led by Li Yimeng[16] to Yugoslavia and Romania from 31 March to 10 April 1978, the Hong Kong and Macau Economy and Trade Investigation Group led by Duan Yun[17] from 10 April to 6 May 1978 and the Chinese Economic Delegation led by Vice-Premier Gu Mu to five countries in Western Europe between 2 May and 6 June 1978 (Han 2011).

The Economic Delegation to Japan reported their findings at a Politburo meeting on 1 June 1978 and proposed to learn from Japan's experience and bring in advanced foreign technologies. The Hong Kong and Macau Economy and Trade Investigation Group reported their findings at a Politburo meeting on 3 June 1978 and proposed establishing special zones as production bases for exports. In 1977, Hong Kong's imports and exports were US$19.6 billion, while mainland China's were US$14.8 billion. The 25 member delegation led by Gu Mu visited France, West Germany, Switzerland, Denmark and Belgium to study Western economies, and they were shocked by the high living standard of ordinary people in these countries. The delegation completed their report in ten days after the trip and reported their findings to the Politburo on 30 June 1978. The Politburo members were so touched by the report that the meeting lasted from 3:30 pm to 11 pm (Liu 2014; Yuan 2017). Following their report to the Politburo, the State Council held a Four Modernization Plan Discussion Conference from 6 July to 9 September 1978 to discuss how to introduce foreign technologies and capital. Li Xiannian, Vice-Chairman of the CPC Central Committee and Vice-Premier of the State Council, announced at the closing session that China would import goods and equipment worth of US$18 billion between 1978 and 1985 (Li 2010).

The top leaders of the CPC also visited developed capitalist countries or East European Countries. Hua Guofeng visited Romania and Yugoslavia from 15 to 29 August 1978 and became interested in their management of enterprises and use of foreign investment and foreign loans for economic development (Zhu 2008). Deng Xiaoping visited Japan from 22 to 29 October 1978; toured Nippon Steel, Panasonic and Nissan Automobiles; and rode the bullet train. While visiting the car manufacturer, Deng Xiaoping remarked "now I know what modernization is" (Liu 2018). During 5–14 November 1978, Deng Xiaoping visited Thailand, Malaysia and Singapore; he was very impressed by Singapore's achievement in economic growth (Leng and Wang 2004). Vice-Premier Wang Zhen visited the UK from 6 to 17 November 1978, and he was surprised by the living standard of ordinary workers and the social welfare. He remarked that he would consider the UK a communist society had it been led by a communist party (Xin 2008;

Liu 2014). The leadership realized by then that China had fallen far behind not only the Western industrialized nations and Japan but also the new industrial powers of Asia, the so-called four tigers, South Korea, Singapore, Taiwan and Hong Kong. At that time China's citizens had to make do with barely sufficient food supplies, rationed clothing, inadequate housing and a service sector that was inadequate and inefficient.

The new leadership was a cohabitation between two camps, the veteran revolutionaries who had been prominent during the civil war and the pragmatic new elites (including some veteran revolutionaries) who were promoted by Mao Zedong during the Cultural Revolution. Although they shared the common goal of modernizing China, they differed on how to deal with the legacy of Mao Zedong. Hua Guofeng and his supporters, the new elites, advocated in February 1977 that the CPC should follow whatever Mao had decided or instructed (the "two whatevers"). The advocacy of the two whatevers by Hua and some of his supporters might be simply tactical, because in some sense the legitimacy of their status came from Mao's decision. After they had arrested Mao's widow and his protégés, they needed Mao's mantle to fend off criticisms from those loyal to Mao Zedong. Had they truly believed the two whatevers they would have blocked Deng Xiaoping's rehabilitation. To the veteran revolutionaries who were humiliated and purged by Mao Zedong during the Cultural Revolution, the two whatevers, which implied that they should not be rehabilitated politically, did not conform to Marxism (Deng 1983). As more and more veteran cadres returned to senior government and CPC positions, the balance of power between the two camps changed, and the veteran revolutionaries became unwilling to let the new elites stay in the driving seat. The debates on the criterion of truth triggered by the publication of the article "Practice Is the Sole Criterion for Testing Truth" in *Guangming Daily* on 11 May 1978 and reprinted by *People's Daily* on the following day became a rallying call for rectifying the legacy of Mao Zedong and removing the new elites from key CPC and government positions. The future General Secretary of the CPC Hu Yaobang[18] was behind its publication (Schoenhals 1991).

The new elite camp found the article too provocative. Wang Dongxing,[19] who was Hua Guofeng's most important supporter, accused the article of being "theoretically absurd, ideologically reactionary and politically banner-cutting". The *Liberation Army Daily* published on 24 June 1978 another article, "A Basic Principle of Marxism", in support of the earlier article, with backing from Senior General Luo Ruiqing who was Secretary General of the CPC Central Military Committee. Deng Xiaoping and most central and provincial leaders began to openly support the view expressed by the two articles between June and October 1978. The veteran revolutionary camp won the ideological battle and got ready to remove the new elites from key positions and further rectify Mao Zedong's legacy. The Central Committee Work Conference of the CPC held from 10 November to 15 December 1978 deviated from its scheduled topics (agricultural production, national economic plans for 1979 and 1980, and Li Xiannian's speech at the State Council's Four Modernization Plan Discussion Conference) following Chen Yun's speech at the Northeast Group Discussion on 12 November 1978 and became a conference to correct past wrongs.

Chen Yun, who was one of the five Vice-Chairmen of the CPC Eighth Central Committee and one of the key figures in charge of finance and the economy during the 1950s and early 1960s, proposed to rehabilitate the 5 April Movement and many prominent CPC figures who were purged by Mao Zedong during and before the Cultural Revolution. His proposal received enthusiastic responses from many participants, and the conference shifted its focus to discussing and correcting past and current mistakes, including Mao Zedong's purge decisions and Hua Guofeng's two whatevers. The conference prepared the milestone Third Plenum of the Eleventh Central Committee of the CPC. On 13 December 1978, Deng Xiaoping delivered a closing speech, "Emancipate the Mind, Seek Truth from Facts, Unite and Look Forward", in which he called for increasing the decision-making power of local governments, firms and production teams and strengthening responsibility systems (Yu 1998a, 1998b). Both camps reached consensus on these ideas for the economy after top leaders and government delegations had visited Yugoslavia, Romania, Japan and Western Europe.

Although the Third Plenum held during 18–22 December 1978 is thought to mark the beginning of China's reform and opening, it is more significant politically and ideologically than economically as economic development had actually, if not officially, become the main work focus of the CPC by 1977. Hua Guofeng and his supporters had no substantial difference with Deng Xiaoping and his supporters in terms of economic policies at the time. Actually, Hua Guofeng announced at the Central Committee Work Conference on 10 November 1978 (the opening day) that the entire party's work focus would shift to socialist construction for modernization from 1 January 1979 (Han 2011). However, Hua Guofeng's supporters were all effectively removed from key positions at the Plenum, so his influence was severely weakened. Deng Xiaoping and his supporters in fact took the helm from Hua Guofeng. Chen Yun was re-elected to the Vice-Chairman position. The CPC leaders decided to officially shift the work focus from class struggle to economic development and modernizing the country (Zhang 1998).

Except more investment and giving more decision-making power to firms and production teams, the leadership had no clear roadmap for future economic development. Therefore, economic policies usually lagged behind grassroots initiatives, one of which, the household production responsibility system (i.e. fixing households' output quotas) in the late 1970s, fundamentally influenced China's reform process. Primitive farming technology, relatively scarce land resources, and the huge surplus of rural labour then in China meant that fixing a household's output quota from its assigned farmland was the appropriate production management approach. This system provided adequate incentives for farmers' efforts in villages that did not have enough CBTEs to absorb the surplus labour. When a plot can be tilled by 2 farmers, assigning ten farmers on it will result in less output because covert freeriding discourages effort. When everyone tries to do less covertly, it leads to the prisoner's dilemma,[20] and not enough food for all the farmers. Fixing households' output quotas was tried spontaneously by farmers and grassroots cadres in many regions with good results since 1956 when advanced cooperatives were widely formed. However, many people involved were accused of walking on the capitalist road and persecuted (Du 2000). During the famine in the early 1960s, the practice was widely used by farmers to overcome the difficulties. The practice was discontinued when food shortages were alleviated in 1962, because Mao Zedong considered it capitalist. The practice was then strictly prohibited until Mao Zedong's death.

Because of the hardship in China's rural areas and the proved effectiveness of fixing households' output quota, many production teams in several provinces secretly assigned farmland to individual households for fixed quotas of grains or cotton after Mao's death. The earliest reported case in the 1970s was Gaolongchen village, Wenchang city, Hainan Administrative District[21] in the winter of 1976 (Li et al. 2008). There were also several cases in other provinces well before the much-publicized cases in Anhui Province (Chen, Chang, and Yuan 2019; Pan 2008; Zhang, Zhang, and Shi 2008; Wang, Li, and Liang 2004). The CPC Anhui Provincial Committee led by First Secretary Wan Li made the *Decisions on Several Issues in Current Rural Policies* in November 1977, giving greater autonomy in farming to production teams, allowing them to assign production responsibility to individuals and encouraging farmers to run family sideline business. In September 1978, the CPC Anhui Provincial Committee decided to allow collective-owned land to be lent to farmers as a relief measure against the severe drought, if the land could not be cultivated by the collectives. This policy soon led to stealthily dividing the land and fixing the output quota to each household by many production teams. On 15 September, Tang Maolin, the CPC Party Secretary of Shannan district, Feixi county, held a meeting at Huanghua village and made the decision to assign farmland to households, which was implemented on 18 September 1978. On 23 September Xiaojingzhuang village divided its farmland, livestock and tools among households

(Ma 2009). They were almost two months earlier than the most famous Xiaogang village, Fengyang city, Anhui Province, which decided to have household production responsibility on 14 November 1978 (Liu 2009). Those grassroots initiatives were well ahead of the Third Plenum of the CPC Central Committee.

China's economy in the late 1970s was far from reaching the potential of a centrally planned economy as its GDP per capita was far below those of the Soviet Union and East European countries. The central planning system in China was generally able to maintain a reasonably high growth rate if there had not been disruptions caused by political campaigns and economic mismanagement. China's GDP decreased by 1.6% in 1976 because of political campaigns during which Deng Xiaoping was purged. The CPC policy under Hua Guofeng to stabilize the country during 1977–1978 was successful. Between 1976 and 1978, China's economy quickly recovered. Industrial output jumped by 14% in 1977 and by 13% in 1978. A third consecutive year of adverse weather conditions led to sluggish agricultural production in 1977, but 1978 saw a record harvest (National Bureau of Statistics of China 1979).

1.3 The adjustment and reform during 1979–1981

The ten-year plan was still a product of the central planning system. It soon proved to be overambitious, and government finance would have a large deficit to implement it. On 14 March 1979, Li Xiannian and Chen Yun wrote to the CPC Central Committee, proposing 1) establishing a State Council Financial and Economic Committee with Chen Yun as director and Li Xiannian as deputy director, and 2) adjusting national economy to solve the severe imbalance. The Politburo held meetings from 21 to 23 March 1979 and decided to adjust national economy and set up the Financial and Economic Committee which would start working immediately to direct the adjustment. The Financial and Economic Committee was formally approved and established on 1 July 1979 by the Ninth Meeting of the Standing Committee of the Fifth National People's Congress.

The CPC Central Committee Work Conference held from 5 to 28 April 1979 adopted an Eight Character (调整、改革、整顿、提高) Guiding Principle to adjust, reform, consolidate and improve the national economy in three years. Its major goals were 1) to address the imbalance between light and heavy industry by increasing the growth rate of agriculture and light industry and reducing investment in heavy industry, and 2) to overcome key deficiencies in transportation, communications, coal, iron, steel, building materials and electric power. The CPC Central Committee and the government also began to reform the operation of agriculture and industrial enterprises and the main ideas were to increase the decision-making power of enterprises and reward good performance (Xie 1983; Zhang 2010; Sun 1999), which was still within the realm of what the Soviet Union and East European Countries had practiced since the 1950s (Schroeder 1990; Balassa 1970; Sapir 1980).

The practice of household production responsibility in rural areas moved well ahead of the agricultural policies of the CPC Central Committee. When the phenomenon of dividing farmland and fixing household output quotas was reported to the CPC Anhui Provincial Committee, Wan Li approved it for trial in early 1979. Because of Wan's support, it later became the most successful reform policy (Wu 1996; Pan 2018), while such grassroots initiatives in other provinces were suppressed or carried on unnoticed. The responsibility system allowed individual households to work a piece of land for profit in return for delivering a set amount of produce to the collective at a given price, creating strong incentives for farmers to reduce production costs and increase productivity. In March 1980, Wan Li was appointed Director of the State Agricultural Commission which was in charge of agricultural reform. The Agricultural Commission drafted the CPC Central Committee Document No. 75 in 1980 *Issues on Further Strengthening and Improving Agricultural Production Responsibility System*, making it the formal policy. Agricultural production was also boosted by allowing some families to operate as "specialized households", devoting their efforts to producing a scarce commodity or service on a profit-making basis (Han 2009).

Concerning industry, on 13 July 1979 the State Council issued five documents on 1) increasing the autonomy of SOE managers, 2) allowing enterprises to keep a proportion of their profits, 3) levying fixed asset tax, 4) increasing the depreciation rate of fixed assets and 5) using loans for the full quantity of cash flow (previously SOE's working capital relied on fiscal appropriation). On 9 August 1980, the State Council issued the report of the State Economic Commission which allowed enterprises to produce unplanned goods for sale on the market and to experiment with the use of bonus to reward higher productivity. Some SOEs started to try production responsibility systems similar to those in agriculture in 1980. The National Work Conference on Industry and Transportation, organized by the State Council and held in Shanghai between 15 and 25 April 1981, called for implementation of Industrial Production Responsibility System. The State Economic Commission and the State Council Institutional Reform Office jointly released *Notes on Issues in Implementation of Industrial Production Responsibility System* on 29 October 1981 and the State Council released the *Provisional Regulations on Issues in Implementing Industrial Production Responsibility System* on 11 November 1981.

The capital construction investment projects used to be funded by government budgetary appropriation, which carried no interest and need not be repaid. On 28 August 1979, the State Council approved and issued the *Report on Trial Use of Loans for Capital Construction Investment* and the *Proposed Regulation on Capital Construction Loans* submitted by the State Planning Commission, the State Construction Commission and the Ministry of Finance. Provincial governments and ministries were instructed to experiment with bank loans for capital construction and accumulate experience for expanding the scheme. The government also tested a fundamental change in financial procedures with a limited number of state-owned units in 1980, and allowed these enterprises to pay a tax on their profits and retain the balance for reinvestment and distribution to workers as bonus. On 5 September 1981, the State Council approved and released the *Ideas on Reforming Industrial and Commercial Tax Regimes* from the Ministry of Finance, which became one of the regulatory documents for changing profit delivery to tax remission.

With the end of Educated Urban Youth Settling in Mountainous and Rural Areas in 1980 and the return to cities of earlier participants of the movement from 1978, urban unemployment became more severe and had to be addressed urgently. The government actively encouraged the establishment of (small-sized) collectively owned industrial and service enterprises as a means of soaking up the unemployed urban population, especially young people. Many SOEs set up collectively owned firms to employ unemployed family members of their employees and earn income for the welfare of their employees. These collectively owned firms set up by SOEs often profited at the expense of their state-owned business, which was the beginning of managers and employees aligning their own interests with their efforts by transferring SOE profits and assets to themselves.

Peddlers, vendors and merchants trading across different cities, which were thought to be capitalist elements and often persecuted in Mao Zedong's era, were more tolerated. In many regions they were encouraged by local governments as a measure to reduce urban unemployment. The first license for individual enterprise was issued in 1980 in Wenzhou, which later became a city with a thriving private economy. The CPC Central Committee Document No. 75 in 1980 stipulated that individuals were not allowed to hire workers. Many successful individual enterprises soon started to hire workers, which triggered a debate in 1981 on whether hiring workers by individual entrepreneurs was exploitation. On 7 July 1981, the State Council issued *Policy Provisions on Urban Non-Agricultural Individual Economy*, stipulating that individual enterprises could employ one or two helpers and those with skills or special expertise could have two to three but no more than five apprentices after approval of the Industry and Commerce Administration.

The growth of private enterprises was also largely due to individual or grassroots initiatives. The role of the senior leaders lies more in their progressively reduced hindrance to entrepreneurship and grassroots initiatives than any active contribution. Entrepreneurs were constantly worried about whether the CPC would persecute them later because of their enterprising activities. Buying in one place and selling in another place to make a profit was considered illegal even in 1982. On 7 January 1981, the State Council issued the *Instructions on Strengthening Market Management and Cracking Down on Speculation, Profiteering and Smuggling Activities*, which prohibited many business activities carried out by private enterprises. Therefore, many private entrepreneurs affiliated their enterprises to townships or villages to make them appearing collectively owned (Liu and Xie 2000; Zhang 1999; Wu and Huang 1996).

This period saw the emergence of joint-stock system in China, which also appeared long before the relevant policies and legislations made by the central government. The first primitive joint stock cooperative firms in the late 1970s were CBTEs and private enterprises which raised fund through certificates promising dividends according to portions of capital. In 1978, farmers in Jinjiang, Fujian Province set up joint-stock cooperatives, which were nominally affiliated to communes, production brigades or teams to avoid persecution (Xu 1994). In 1979, the first joint-stock cooperative firm in Guangdong Province was set up in Tongqing, Huazhou city (Chen 1998). The first formal joint-stock firm, Chengdu Industrial Exhibition Trust Co., Ltd, was approved by the Chengdu municipal government and established on 15 June 1980 (Xiao 2016). The joint-stock system would fundamentally transform the ownership structure in China's economy.

More progress was made in opening to the outside during this period. Four coastal special export zones were approved on 15 July 1979 by the CPC Central Committee and the State Council as enclaves where foreign investment could receive special treatment. The idea was originated from the report of the Hong Kong and Macau Economy and Trade Investigation Group. They were renamed Special Economic Zones on 16 May 1980, which was approved by the 15th Meeting of the Standing Committee of the Fifth National People's Congress on 26 August 1980 (Wang 2006). Three of the four zones – Shenzhen which is adjacent to Hong Kong, Zhuhai which is adjacent to Macau, and Shantou – were located in Guangdong Province. The fourth, Xiamen, in Fujian Province, was directly across the strait from Taiwan. Foreign trade procedures were eased to allow enterprises and administrative departments outside the Ministry of Foreign Trade to directly negotiate with foreign firms. A dual-track foreign exchange rate system began on 1 January 1981, with an internal settlement rate for trade and an official rate for non-trade settlement. A wide range of cooperation, trade and credit arrangements with foreign firms was legalized to facilitate international trade.

In 1979, the CPC Central Committee and the State Council began to advocate one-child per couple with the slogan "having one is best, at most two". On 25 September 1980, the CPC Central Committee issued *An Open Letter to All Communist Party Members and Communist Youth League Members on the Population Growth of Our Country*, calling for one-child per couple. Soon the government strictly implemented the one-child policy. The policy lasted for 35 years until 29 October 2015 when the Fifth Plenum of the Eighteenth CPC Central Committee decided to end it. The policy might have generated demographic dividend and helped the growth of China's GDP per capita, but it also accelerated China's population aging. It would have severe implications for China's future economy (Feng, Gu, and Cai 2016; Feng, Cai, and Gu 2013).

The adjustment achieved its objectives to shrink investment in heavy industry and promote growth in agriculture and light industry. During the period of adjustment, all sectors of the economy showed strong growth except heavy industry. Agricultural production was stimulated in 1979 by an increase of over 22% in the procurement prices paid for farm products. Incomes of ordinary citizens, especially farmers, increased substantially; the supply of food and other consumer goods also increased noticeably, even though many goods still required ration coupons in cities. The GDP growth in 1979, 1980 and 1981 was 7.6%, 7.81% and 5.17% respectively. The government finance turned from a surplus of CNY 1.017 billion in 1978 to a deficit of CNY 13.541 billion in 1979 and CNY 6.89 billion in 1980. Consumers had the first experience of a wide range price increase since the Cultural Revolution. Government finance returned to a surplus of CNY 3.738 billion in 1981 (National Bureau of Statistics of China 1980, 1981, 1982).

The future path of China's reform and opening was delimited by Deng Xiaoping in a speech entitled "Adhere to the Four Cardinal Principles" on 30 March 1979 at the National Theoretical Work Discussion Conference organized by the CPC Central Committee and held in Beijing between 18 January and 3 April 1979. The Four Cardinal Principles are adherence to socialist road, adherence to people's democratic dictatorship (i.e. proletarian dictatorship), adherence to the leadership of the Communist Party (i.e. control of the government and the country by the CPC) and adherence to Marxism-Leninism-Mao Zedong Thought. Deng Xiaoping proclaimed that the Four Cardinal Principles were the fundamental prerequisite for China to achieve Four Modernizations (Party Literature Research Center of the CPC Central Committee 1989; Wang 2014). In a conversation on 16 September

1993, Deng Xiaoping noted that the core of the Four Cardinal Principles was the leadership of the Communist Party, and the superiority of the socialist market economy relied on adherence to the Four Cardinal Principles (Pan 2010; Ni 2014). Deng's Four Cardinal Principles drew a red line for China's reform.

While the utopian Mao Zedong wanted to realize communism rapidly by instilling communist spirit into people and worried about that private entrepreneurship would lead to capitalist restoration, the pragmatist Deng Xiaoping understood that China needs a strong economy. Although Deng Xiaoping has been depicted as the chief architect of China's reform and opening by official narratives, he did not propose any original reform schemes. However, unlike some of his fellow veteran revolutionaries who were burdened by Mao's worry about capitalist restoration, Deng Xiaoping viewed socialism as solid control of the country by the CPC. Therefore, he would allow any initiatives that help China's economic growth, as long as they would not undermine the leadership of the CPC or weaken government control over strategically important industries (i.e. socialist road). If Deng Xiaoping did design something, it was the forbidden zone which reform could not touch, but he also left the remaining areas for market and private entrepreneurship.

1.4   Deepening reform: 1982–1991

On the strength of the initial successes, especially in agriculture, the CPC leadership decided to broaden the reform program and make "reform and opening" China's fundamental policy. The Twelfth National Congress of the CPC defined China's economy as a Planned Economy Supplemented by Market Regulation, which shows that the leadership still believed in central planning as the main policy tool to manage economy. The Organization Department of the CPC Central Committee implemented a cadre appraisal system in 1979 which emphasizes measurable achievement as well as political stand and ideological quality. During the 1980s, the appraisal system evolved more toward measurable achievements in contributing to local economic growth, such as improved GDP growth rate, new development projects and foreign investments attracted, which would help an official's career progression (Quan 2004; Deng 1995; Wang 1986). The CPC and government officials have become extremely pro-business and often use government resources to help business developers when local residents object to a development project.

The agricultural reform progressed fast and smoothly, and the main obstacles were ideology from Mao Zedong's era and CPC cadres with such ideology. On 1 January 1982, the CPC Central Committee issued No. 1 Document in 1982, the *Minutes of National Work Conference on Rural Areas*, which endorsed various forms of the contract responsibility system in agriculture, including dividing collectively owned land among households with fixed output quota. On 1 January 1983, the CPC Central Committee issued No. 1 Document in 1983, *Issues in Current Rural Economic Policy*, stating that the household contract responsibility system was a great innovation of Chinese farmers under the leadership of the CPC and it was a new development of the Marxist agricultural cooperation theory in its practice in China. The household contract responsibility system was adopted as the organizational norm for the entire country.

As the new constitution approved at the Fifth Meeting of the Fifth National People's Congress on 4 December 1982 stipulates that the lowest level of local government is the township government, the people's communes no longer have the legal basis to be both a level of government and the management of cooperatives. The CPC Central Committee and the State Council jointly issued the *Notice on Separating Administration from Cooperative Management and Establishing Township Government* on 12 October 1983, and villager committees would become the grassroots autonomous administration to help township government manage villages. On 1 January 1984, the CPC Central Committee No. 1 Document in 1984, *Notice on 1984 Rural Work,* stipulated that the contract for land in the household contract responsibility system should be longer than 15 years and even longer for long production cycle or developmental projects. By the end of 1984, all but a handful of people's communes had been dissolved.

The agricultural reform between 1978 and 1984 was a stunning success. Grain output increased from around 200 million tons in 1978 to 407.12 million tons in 1984 (in which chemical fertilizers also played a key role) and the average per capita net income of farmers from CNY 133.57 in 1978 to CNY 355.33 in 1984 (National Bureau of Statistics of China 1979, 1985). On 1 January 1985, the CPC Central Committee No. 1 Document in 1985, *Ten Policies on Further Activation of Rural Economy,* repealed the system of unified and fixed state purchase of agricultural and sideline products, and implemented a new system of state planned contractual purchase of key products such as grains and cotton. On 1 January 1986, the CPC Central Committee No. 1 Document in 1986 confirmed that the rural reform policies were correct and would continue to be implemented.

The industrial production responsibility system enforced from the end of 1981 and the earlier reform measures did not bring about the kind of dramatic improvement that the responsibility system achieved in agriculture. Nonetheless the new policies significantly increased opportunities available to most enterprises. Managers gained greater control over their enterprises including the right to hire and fire. Premier Zhao Ziyang's Report on the Sixth Five-Year Plan was approved by the Fifth Meeting of the Fifth National People's Congress on 10 December 1982, which indicated the nationwide implementation of changing profit delivery to tax remission in 1983. With the first stage of changing profit delivery to tax remission in 1983, SOEs still had to hand a part of the after-tax profits to the state. With its second stage implemented in 1984, 11 types of tax for SOEs are levied and SOEs no longer need to hand their after-tax profits to the state.

SOE managers wanted more power. As the finance and accounting system then played the supervisory role and served as a check on the managers, they felt they were being tied. On 24 March 1984, backed by Xiang Nan, First Secretary of the CPC Fujian Provincial Committee, *Fujian Daily* published an open letter "Please Untie Us" from 55 SOE managers in Fujian Province appealing for more power to enable them to contribute more to the socialist economic construction. *People's Daily* reprinted the letter on 30 March 1984, resulting in nationwide discussion and giving new impetus to the SOE reform. On 10 May 1984, the State Council issued the *Provisional Regulation on Further Increasing Autonomy of State-Run Industrial Enterprises*, giving 1) SOE managers the authority to hire and fire workers, to reward workers with bonus and to fine workers and 2) SOEs the right to price and sell extra products at market after they have completed state-planned output.

With the immense success of reform in rural areas, the CPC Central Committee decided to move its work focus to reforming the economic system in cities and issued *Decision on the Reform of Economic System* approved at the Third Plenum of the Twelfth Central Committee of the CPC on 20 October 1984. The document defined China's economy as planned commodity economy on the basis of public ownership. The practice of remitting taxes on profits and retaining the balance became universal by 1985, increasing the incentive for enterprises to maximize profits. The capital investment projects became all funded by interest-bearing bank loans from the beginning of 1985. On 12 July 1986, the State Council released four documents on reforming the labour system, replacing the lifetime employment with a labour contract system and establishing unemployment insurance, which began to be implemented on 1 October 1986. With the introduction of the labour contract system, managers of the SOEs obtained greater control over their firms. On 13 April 1988, the First Meeting of the Seventh National People's Congress approved the *Law of People's Republic of China on Industrial Enterprise of the Ownership by the Whole People*, which establishes the manager responsibility system and the autonomy of SOEs in their operation.

Fourteen coastal cities, Dalian, Qinhuangdao, Tianjin, Yantai, Qingdao, Lianyungang, Nantong, Ningbo, Wenzhou, Fuzhou, Shanghai, Zhanjiang, Guangzhou and Beihai, were designated coastal open cities by the CPC Central Committee and the State Council in April and announced on 4 May

1984. These cities were to create productive exchanges between foreign firms with advanced technology and major Chinese economic networks (Wang 1986). The internal settlement foreign exchange rate for trade was abolished on 1 January 1985, but a market-determined foreign exchange swap rate was used in parallel with the official rate, establishing a formal dual-track foreign exchange rate system (Bi et al. 2013). The volume of international trade grew rapidly, and so did the combined value of imports and exports as the share of GDP, which had seldom exceeded 10% of national income before 1978. It reached 15% in 1980, 21% in 1984 and 35% in 1986. Textiles were the leading export category; petroleum and foodstuffs were also important exports. Leading imports included machinery, transport equipment, manufactured goods, and chemicals. Restrictions on trade were loosened further in the mid-1980s, and foreign investment including sole ownership by foreign investors was legalized. The most common foreign investments were joint ventures between foreign firms and Chinese enterprises, especially SOEs.

Private entrepreneurship and free market activities at rural and urban fairs were legalized and encouraged in the 1980s, but there were serious differences among the CPC leadership on what should be allowed. Grassroots initiatives again proceeded ahead of the CPC policies and became targets for cracking down. On 13 April 1982, the CPC Central Committee and the State Council issued the *Decision on Cracking Down Severe Criminal Activities in Economic Field*, targeting long-distance transport for trade, speculation, profiteering and smuggling. The cracking down was loosened before long. The CPC Central Committee No. 1 Document in 1983, *Issues in Current Rural Economic Policy,* permitted private enterprises to conduct long-distance transport for trade, to buy large or medium-size vehicles and to be engaged in commerce. On 22 January 1987, the CPC Central Committee Document No. 5 in 1987, *Deepening Rural Reform*, formally acknowledged that rural individual enterprise owners could hire one or two helpers and those with skills could have three to five apprentices, which were exceeded already. The State Council issued in 25 June 1988 the *Provisional Regulations of the People's Republic of China on Private Enterprises* which was implemented on 1 July 1988, removing the hiring restriction on private enterprises. A rapidly growing private and collectively owned system enlivened the domestic commerce, and competed vigorously with the state-owned commercial agencies and retail outlets, providing a wider range of consumption choices for Chinese citizens than at any previous time.

The Thirteenth National Congress of the CPC held from 25 October to 1 November 1987 espoused the theory of the primary stage of socialism and called for the construction of socialism with Chinese characteristics. The First Meeting of the Seventh National People's Congress approved the plan to make the island Hainan a province and the largest special economic zone on 13 April 1988. Deng Xiaoping and the CPC leadership thought that it was the time to remove price control, and he was quoted as saying, "long pain is worse than short pain" and reform must break through the "price pass". Official media began to prepare public opinion on the necessity of breaking through the price pass (Yang 2009). On 5 April 1988, the State Council announced to lift price control over pork, eggs, sugar and common vegetables, and to give employees non-staple food subsidies by their employers along with their wages. The price of color television sets was allowed to float 20% above the state-planned price after May 1988. The State Council announced to lift price control over 13 famous brands of cigarettes and spirits on 28 July 1988, and their prices increased around ten times on that day. On 19 August 1988, the Central People's Broadcasting Station reported the news that the Preliminary Scheme on Price and Wage Reform had been approved in principle by the Tenth Plenary Meeting of the CPC Central Committee Politburo held between 15 and 17 August 1988. The news triggered a wave of nationwide panic buying. People bought almost every consumer good in large quantities, so prices of goods in severe short supply such as colour television and refrigerators rocketed.

Because of the rampant price increase, the 20th Executive Meeting of the State Council on 30 August 1988 decided to improve price management and stabilize the market, cease to adjust prices in the rest of the year, introduce inflation-proof bank deposits, reduce the scale of capital construction, control money issuance and ensure commodity supply. The Work Meeting of the CPC Central Committee Politburo on 23 September 1988 decided to rectify and consolidate. The Third Plenum of the Thirteenth Central Committee of the CPC formally approved the guidelines of "rectifying the economic environment, consolidating the economic order and deepening the all-round reform" (Party Literature Research Center of the CPC Central Committee 2005; Yang 2009). The rectification and consolidation was a contractionary policy intended to fight inflation. The retail price index (RPI) increased 18.5% in 1988 and 17.8% in 1989. The discontent toward high inflation and profiteering by people with government connections from the dual-price system, which was gradually implemented since 1979 as transition to a full market–determined price system, led to student protests in Beijing and other cities in April and May and martial law in Beijing from 20 May 1989. The protests in Beijing ended on 4 June 1989 with the martial law enforcing troops taking control of Tiananmen Square in Beijing. At the time, Deng Xiaoping was Chairman of the Central Military Committee of the CPC and Chairman of the State Military Committee of China, the supreme commander in China's military system.

Although the "crossing price pass" attempt was considered a failure, it moved the price level closer to or above the normal market-determined price and prepared the general public psychologically for future price reform, paving the way to market pricing. The Fifth Plenum of the Thirteenth Central Committee of the CPC passed the *Decision on Further Rectification, Consolidation and Deepening Reform* on 9 November 1989. Firmer and stricter measures were taken to reduce government spending, money issuance, bank credit and capital construction to prevent citizen's income from increasing too fast and to inhibit excessive consumer demand. The inflation was under control by 1990 at the expense of economic growth, with the RPI increasing 2.1% in 1990 and 2.9% in 1991. The GDP growth rate dropped from 11.3% in 1988 to 4.1% in 1989 and 3.8% in 1990, and recovered to 9.2% in 1991. With the sluggish market between 1989 and 1991, more inappropriate prices were adjusted, which stimulated production and supply of commodities. The difference between the state-planned prices and the market prices became smaller, creating the condition for lifting all price controls.

Pudong Development and Opening started in this period. Developing Pudong was first proposed in 1984 in the *Report Outline on Shanghai's Economic Development Strategy* prepared by the Shanghai government and the State Council Shanghai Rebuilding and Revitalizing Research Group. The report was approved by the State Council on 8 February 1985. A Joint Research and Consulting Group for Developing Pudong, consisting of home and overseas experts, was set up by the Shanghai government in June 1987. The Shanghai government organized an International Symposium on Pudong New Area Development during 2–4 May 1988, with over 140 home and overseas participants, including representatives from the World Bank and the Asia Development Bank. The CPC Shanghai Committee and Shanghai government submitted a *Report on Developing Pudong* to the CPC Central Committee in February 1989. Deng Xiaoping spent Chinese New Year in Shanghai in January 1990 and local leaders reported the Pudong development plan to him and won his support. When he returned to Beijing in February 1990, he asked the Politburo to support the plan. In China's political environment, although Deng Xiaoping had retired from all his official positions, he still exerted greater influence on the decision-making of the CPC Central Committee than those in top positions. Premier Li Peng announced on 18 April 1990 that the CPC Central Committee and the State Council had approved the Pudong area in Shanghai as a new economic development zone with more privileges than other special economic zones, allowing foreign investors to open financial institutions, department stores and supermarkets.

More joint-stock firms were formed through new investments or transformation of existing firms during 1982–1991. Various forms of shares were issued within and outside the joint-stock firms. Since demand for financial assets depends on their liquidity, that is, the ability to be converted into cash, growth in share issuance requires a market to trade shares. Soon private trading of shares appeared in different cities, although it was deemed illegal by the authorities. Shenzhen Special Economic Zone Securities Company was approved by the People's Bank of China (PBOC) in September 1985 to operate on a trial basis. On 26 September 1986, the Jingan Office of the Industrial and Commercial Bank of China (ICBC) Shanghai Trust and Investment Company opened the first approved share trading counter. Shenzhen Special Economic Zone Securities Company opened Shenzhen's first approved share trading counter on 7 April 1987. Formally established on 26 September 1987, it was the first securities company in China since 1949. In 1988, over 30 securities companies were established across the country. The CPC Central Committee and the State Council usually approved grassroots initiatives on joint-stock firms and securities years afterwards. By 1990, around 4750 enterprises issued shares of various forms and raised CNY 4.201 billion. Over 3200 enterprises were transformed into joint-stock firms by the end of 1991 (Xiao 2016). The Shanghai Stock Exchange opened on 26 November 1990 and the Shenzhen Stock Exchange opened on 1 December 1990. The companies listed on the two exchanges initially were mainly UCOEs and SOEs that need capital injection.

1.5   Creating a socialist market economy: 1992–2001

The contractionary economic policy since late 1988 and the political events during 1989–1991 in China, Eastern Europe and the Soviet Union led to confusion in the CPC and the society about the direction and pace of China's reform. During a visit to southern China from 18 January to 21 February 1992, Deng Xiaoping made a series of political pronouncements designed to give new impetus to the process of economic reform. The Politburo of the CPC Central Committee held a plenary meeting on 9 and 10 March 1992 and agreed totally with the opinions expressed by Deng Xiaoping during his trip. A new round of capital investment and economic boom began. The 14th National Congress of the CPC during 12–18 October 1992 also backed Deng's pronouncements and stated that China's key task in the 1990s was to create a "Socialist Market Economy". The State Council issued *The Notice Regarding Implementation of System of National Accounting* in August 1992, so the Western System of National Accounting (SNA) officially replaced the Soviet Union's Material Product System (MPS) and GDP became China's most important economic indicator. On 11 October 1992, the State Council approved the establishment of the Pudong New Area in Shanghai. The State Council lifted more price controls, especially over capital materials and agricultural products in 1992. With consecutive years of bumper harvests and high levels of grain storage, 844 counties or county-level cities lifted price control over grains at the end of 1992. The GDP growth rate was 14.2% in 1992, while the inflation rate was 6.4%.

On 18 March 1993, the State Council issued the *Notice on Accelerating the Reform of Food Circulation System*, abolishing grain coupons and the grain and edible oil supply system for urban residents. By 1993 the two price tracks for iron and steel products and most engineering goods had merged into one market pricing mechanism. During 1993 and 1994, the output continued to grow fast, prices were increasing, and investment outside the state budget was soaring. Economic expansion was fuelled by the introduction of more special economic or technological development zones, the influx of foreign capital that those special zones facilitated and the phenomenal growth of private and township and village enterprises (TVEs, previously CBTEs). The GDP growth rate was 14% in 1993, while the inflation rate jumped to 14.7% in 1993.

Fearing hyperinflation, the CPC Central Committee and the State Council issued the *Opinions on Current Economic Situation and Strengthening Macroeconomic Control* on 24 June 1993. The government raised interest rates, re-evaluated investment projects, and ordered banks to call back speculative loans and reduce lending. In 1993 the CPC Central Committee decided to adopt a tax system of revenue sharing between central and local governments. The State Council released six provisional regulations on value-added tax, consumption tax, business tax, business income tax, resource tax and land appreciation tax on 13 December 1993 and issued the *Decision on Implementing Tax Sharing Fiscal Administrative System* on 25 December 1993. These regulations became effective on 1 January 1994. However, the GDP growth rate was still 13.1% in 1994 with the inflation rate reaching 24.1%. The tax-sharing system greatly enhanced the financial strength of the central government and reduced the proportion of national income controlled by the local governments which bear the lion's share of government responsibilities. With all the anti-inflation measures the government implemented, the inflation rate gradually dropped to 17% in 1995 and to 8% in early 1996. As the Asian Financial Crisis led to decreased FDI and a sharp drop in China's export growth, the inflation rate decreased to 2.8% in 1997, followed by five years of negative or below 1% inflation rate. China's economy continued to grow at a rapid pace, with its growth rate at 10.9% in 1995, 10% at 1996, 8.9% in 1997, 7.84% in 1998, 7.67% in 1999, 8.49% in 2000 and 8.34% in 2001. China became the second largest economy in terms of purchasing power parity (PPP)[22] in the world after the US in 1999, with its 1.25 billion people and $3800 per capita (PPP). The GDP in 2000 had quadrupled compared with that in 1978.

Although China's economy had grown fast, the increased autonomy and managerial power in SOEs failed to increase their efficiency, productivity and profitability. The leadership and their advisors had not fully grasped the principal–agent problem in corporate governance, so that the reform measures increased SOE managers' power and weakened the check on them by finance and accounting staff without increasing managers' income pertinent to their newly acquired power. Because formal incomes for SOE managers had not increased with their power, they used their new autonomy and power for personal gains. While private enterprises with less capital, worse technologies and fewer technical talents thrived, over half of China's SOEs were reporting losses in the 1990s. The poor performance of SOEs caused massive bad debts in China's banking system.

Since SOEs as a whole made large losses every year in the early 1990s and became a huge financial burden to the government (Sheng et al. 2011; Sheng 2012), the CPC leadership decided to keep control of strategically important enterprises only. The Fifth Plenum of the Fourteenth Central Committee of the CPC held during 25–28 September 1995 proposed the guideline of "grasp the large and let go the small" for reforming SOEs. On 7 March 1996, the State Council approved and released the *Implementation Plan of State Owned Enterprise Reform in 1996* prepared by the State Economic and Trade Commission, calling for supporting and strengthening 1000 state-owned large and medium-sized enterprises and accelerating reform and reorganization of smaller SOEs. During the *15th National Congress* of the CPC held from 12 to 18 September 1997, General Secretary of the CPC and President of the PRC Jiang Zemin announced plans to sell, merge or close the vast majority of SOEs for increased "non-public ownership" in the economy. The 9th National People's Congress endorsed the plans at its first meeting during 5–19 March 1998. Following these decisions, most SOEs were privatized through management buyout or acquisition by private enterprises, with massive layoffs. The majority of SOE managers forced the CPC to privatize SOEs by making huge losses through pursuit of personal enrichment, and most SOEs bought by their managers at symbolic prices often immediately turned profitable. The principal–agent problem of these SOEs was solved mainly by transferring the ownership to their managers.

The banking system has accumulated too many non-performing loans since the 1980s. To increase the capital adequacy ratio of the state-owned banks, the Ministry of Finance issued CNY 270 billion 30 year special bonds with a yearly interest rate of 7.2% to the four largest state-owned banks, ICBC, China Construction Bank (CCB), Bank of China (BOC) and Agricultural Bank of China (ABC), on 18 August 1998 and injected the capital raised from the bonds into these banks. In September 1998, the Ministry of Finance issued CNY 100 billion 10-year bonds with a yearly interest rate of 5.5% to the four state-owned banks. The government set up four asset management companies, Great Wall, Huarong, Orient and Xinda, to strip off bad debts of the four banks and the State Development Bank by buying CNY 1393.9 billion non-performing assets at full book value in 1999. In 2000, China claimed success in its three-year effort to make the majority of large SOEs profitable.

Although houses and apartments began to be sold as commodity in 1979, the accommodation of most urban residents was still provided by their institutions until the late 1990s. The State Council issued the *Notice on Further Deepening Urban Housing System Reform and Accelerating Housing Construction* on 3 July 1998, which stopped the practice of providing urban residents housing by their institutions and made it clear that accommodation would be obtained through market as commodity bought with money. As undeveloped land in urban areas was limited, housing development projects had to demolish existing residential buildings before long. On 13 June 2001, Premier Zhu Rongji signed the *Regulation on the Management of Urban Housing Demolition and Relocation* to be implemented from 1 November 2001, which would become the legal basis for demolishing many urban houses for new housing development projects without consent of their owners.

After six years of hard negotiation and bargaining, on 11 December 2001 China became a member of the World Trade Organization (WTO), for which it formally applied on 11 July 1995. The WTO membership gave its processing trade broader space and a greater chance of development. China's economy grew at an average rate of 10.33% per year during the period 1992–2001. This period transformed China from a public ownership–dominated economy into a mixed economy, in which SOEs control the strategically important sectors as monopoly or oligopoly, while private enterprises thrive in the sectors open to private capital. Managers of medium and small SOEs as well as collectively owned enterprises bought their enterprises at a fraction of the real values, and became the new rich in the socialist market economy. Many workers lost their jobs and the welfare associated with their jobs (Lee 2000; Cai, Park, and Zhao 2008).

1.6   Building a moderately prosperous society: 2002–present

The WTO membership boosted China's exports, which became an important driving force for China's economic growth and accounted for about a quarter of the growth. The foreign exchanges earned by exporters led to increased money supply by the central bank to buy foreign currencies from the exporters and growing foreign exchange reserves. The increased money supply stimulated growth of other sectors including the housing industry. In order to facilitate healthy growth of the real estate industry, the Ministry of Land and Resources issued the *Regulation on Bidding, Auction and Listing for Transferring the Right to Use State Owned Lands* on 9 May 2002, which was implemented on 1 July 2002. Since local governments have more responsibilities and fewer sources of income after the implementation of the tax-sharing system in 1993, they took measures to increase housing demand and house prices, so that they can have more revenues. The Third Plenum of the Sixteenth Central Committee of the CPC held from 11 to 14 October 2003 approved the *Amendments to the Constitution Proposed by the Central Committee of the CPC*, one of which was a proposal to provide protection for private property rights. The Second Meeting of the Tenth National People's Congress approved the amendments on 14 March 2004. From 2004, house prices increased unabatedly for nearly ten years with annual growth rates at around 20%, despite the central government issuing many policies to curb its fast increase. Housing investment became an important driving force in China's economic growth between 2004 and 2013.

Since China promised to let foreign banks fully operate in China at some later date in order to enter the WTO, the state-owned banks needed to be better prepared for the challenge of competing with them. On 6 January 2004, the State Council announced that US$45 billion of foreign exchange reserve had been injected into BOC and CCB (22.5 billion each) by 31 December 2003. On 22 May 2004, BOC and CCB sold CNY 278.7 billion of suspicious loans to Xinda. Xinda and Orient bought non-performing loans of CNY 142.4 billion from BOC, CNY 56.9 billion from CCB and CNY 64 billion from Bank of Communications at full book value. In August 2004, HSBC bought 19.9% of Bank of Communications, the fifth largest state owned bank in China, for US$1.75 billion. It was listed on Hong Kong stock Exchange on 23 June 2005. In April 2005, US$15 billion was injected into ICBC. ICBC sold CNY 246 billion of non-performing assets to Huarong at full book value in May 2005, and auctioned CNY 450 billion of suspicious assets to asset management companies in June 2005. Royal Bank of Scotland took 10% stake in BOC as a strategic partner in August 2005 for US$3.1 billion. Bank of America took a stake in CCB in September 2005. ICBC signed an agreement of strategic investment and cooperation on 27 January 2006 with Goldman Sachs, Allianz and American Express, which together would invest US$3.782 billion in ICBC. On 6 November 2008, Central Huijin Company, a subsidiary of China's Sovereign Wealth Fund, injected CNY 130 billion worth of foreign exchange (US$19 billion) into ABC. Before the initial public offering (IPO) of ABC, the Ministry of Finance bought its CNY 815.7 billion of bad debts with CNY 150.6 billion in cash and CNY 665.1 billion in receivables of the Ministry of Finance.

After stripping-off of bad debts and injection of capital, the five largest state owned banks were all listed on Hong Kong Stock Exchange and Shanghai Stock Exchange.

While the WTO membership boosted exports, the housing and construction industry became another key source of economic growth after 2001. China's GDP grew at an average rate of 11.26% between 2002 and 2007 with an increasing trend. The growth rate was 9.13% in 2002 and 14.23% in 2007 despite attempts by the government to cool the economy. China's total trade in 2006 surpassed US$1.76 trillion, making China the third-largest trading nation after the US and Germany. China's GDP stood at US$3.55 trillion in 2007, making China the third largest economy after the US and Japan. The 2008 financial crisis in the US and Europe had a negative impact on China's growth rate, which was still at 9.65% in 2008. On 5 November 2008, the State Council Executive Meeting presided by Premier Wen Jiabao decided to carry out a CNY 4 trillion stimulus package by the end of 2010. The stimulus package sustained China's fast economic growth, which was 9.40% in 2009, 10.64% in 2010 and 9.54% in 2011. China's GDP of US$6.1 trillion exceeded that of Japan in 2010 and China became the second largest economy in the world.

China's real GDP growth rate drops below 8% since 2012. Its nominal GDP in terms of US dollars totalled approximately US$13.6 trillion in 2018, with a real GDP growth rate 6.6% which is the lowest since 1990. In terms of PPP, China's economy has been the largest in the world since 2016. China is also the world's largest trading power, with a total international trade value of US$4.62 trillion in 2018. Its foreign exchange reserves reached US$3.86 trillion by the end of 2014, making its reserves by far the world's largest. In 2019, *Fortune*'s Global 500 list of the world's largest corporations included 119 Chinese companies. Some of the largest companies in the world were Chinese, including three of the top five on the Global 500 list in 2019 and three of the top four in 2017 and 2018.

1.7   China's rapid growth, Washington Consensus and China Model

From the brief history of China's reform and opening, we can see that China's growth is closely associated with allowing private and foreign enterprises to operate in more and more sectors of the economy. These reforms gradually provide adequate incentives to entrepreneurs, managers, workers and investors. The success of China's economic reform is also a history in which private enterprises grow perseveringly despite unfavourable factors such as the legacy of Mao Zedong's socialist road, whereby the government insists on giving large SOEs privileges and financial support not enjoyed by the private sector. If we view China's reform and opening from a developmental perspective, although China has not fully adopted the recommendations in the Washington Consensus, its policies generally move toward them.

The Washington Consensus has been widely interpreted as offering a policy prescription for wider application than for Latin America. It has also been used as a benchmark in discussing the wider methodological implications of China's economic growth. It includes ten recommendations (Williamson 2004):

1 Budget deficits should be small enough to be financed without recourse to the inflation tax.
2 Public expenditure should be redirected from politically sensitive areas that receive more resources than their economic return can justify toward neglected fields with high economic returns and the potential to improve income distribution, such as primary education and health, and infrastructure.
3 Tax reform to broaden the tax base and cut marginal tax rates.
4 Financial liberalization involving an ultimate objective of market-determined interest rates.
5 A unified exchange rate at a level sufficiently competitive to induce a rapid growth in non-traditional exports.
6 Quantitative trade restrictions to be rapidly replaced by tariffs, which would be progressively reduced until a uniform low rate in the range of 10% to 20% was achieved.
7 Abolition of barriers impeding the entry of FDI.
8 Privatization of state enterprises.
9 Abolition of regulations that impede the entry of new firms or restrict competition.
10 The provision of secure property rights, especially to the informal sector.

From a careful comparison with China's practice since 1978, it seems that what China has done so far is to move from its previous planned economy toward the Washington Consensus rather than away from it. We can examine China's practice in terms of the 10 recommendations:

1 China's budget deficit has been relatively small over the past four decades.
2 China's public expenditure has been generally directed to education, health and infrastructure.
3 China's tax reform has broadened its tax base.

4 China has been liberalizing its financial system with an ultimate objective of market-determined interest rates.

5 China has developed a unified and competitive exchange rate.

6 China has used tariffs to replace its quantitative trade restrictions and reduced its tariff level substantially.

7 China has installed many measures to facilitate FDI.

8 China has privatized most of its SOEs.

9 China has abolished most regulations that impede the entry of new firms in most sectors.

10 China has amended its constitution to protect property rights.

The Washington Consensus does not require implementation of all measures at one go, so that a gradualist approach for some of the measures does not necessarily contradict it.

Although China's success is consistent with, rather than contradictory to, the Washington Consensus, the mainstream economists still need to face the challenge posed by the supporters of the China Model or Beijing Consensus; that is, many countries whose policies were closer to the Washington Consensus than China's performed worse in economic growth. This phenomenon suggests that factors and mechanisms other than those listed in the Washington Consensus play an essential role in China's rapid economic growth. Justin Lin, Angang Hu and Weiwei Zhang are among the most famous proponents of the China Model. Lin, who is usually more vocal in Chinese publications on this topic than in English publications, claims that China's rapid growth could not be explained by Western mainstream economic theory and the key to China's success lies in breaking up the myth of liberalization, privatization and marketization of neoliberalism (Lin 2016, 2017). Angang Hu asserts that "China's rise is rooted in the superiorities of its system" (Hu 2011). Weiwei Zhang concludes that in terms of eradicating poverty, the Chinese model has worked far more effectively than what can be called the American model (Zhang 2006).

1.8 Summary

China's rapid economic growth is primarily driven by the enterprising spirit of ordinary Chinese people, which had been suppressed by the CPC before 1978. Shifting work focus away from class struggle to economic construction after the death of Mao Zedong prepared the path for liberating their enterprising spirit and creativity. Many pragmatic grassroots and senior CPC cadres tried to loosen the suppression and acquiesced in ordinary people's business innovations that had crossed the red line drawn by the contemporaneous CPC policies. Although Deng Xiaoping has been called the chief architect of China's reform and opening, he did not propose any original reform schemes. His main role was being permissive or supportive to policy innovations by lower-level cadres and business innovations by ordinary Chinese people, because he understood that China needed growth and the CPC authority was strong enough to withstand the existence of private enterprises.

Contrary to the popular view that China's growth contradicts the Washington Consensus, China's reform and opening are generally consistent with it. Since many countries with policies closer to the Washington Consensus have not grown as fast as China, other factors might also play a role in China's rapid growth. The supporters of the China Model appear to have a point in emphasizing the role of China's institutions. The claim that modern economics cannot explain China's economic success seems overstretched. To understand China's rapid economic growth, besides mainstream development economics, we need to investigate the role of socio-political, historical and cultural factors as well.

Notes

1 Marshal Lin Biao was Vice-Chairman of the CPC Central Committee, Vice-Premier of the State Council and Minister of Defence. He was No. 2 in the CPC hierarchy during the Cultural Revolution.

2 Chen Jinhua was then Deputy Head of the Planning Group of the Ministry of Light Industry which was formed in July 1970 via the merger of the Ministry of Textile Industry, the Ministry of the First Light Industry and the Ministry of the Second Light Industry.

3 Li Xiannian was then member of the Politburo of the CPC Central Committee, Vice-Premier of the State Council, and Deputy Head of the State Council Working Group which was formed in early 1967 and headed by then Premier Zhou Enlai to oversee the operations of the State Council and the ministries when most ministers and senior officials were toppled by the Cultural Revolution.

4 Hua Guofeng was then Deputy Head of the State Council Working Group and member of the CPC Central Committee.

5 Yu Qiuli was then member of the State Council Working Group, Director of the State Planning Commission and member of the CPC Central Committee.

6 Xiang Nan was then Director of the Agricultural Machinery Bureau of the Ministry of First Machine Building Industry and First Secretary of CPC Fujian Committee from 1982.

7 Four Modernizations are modernized agriculture, industry, defence, and science and technology.

8 A commune oversees many production brigades and a production brigade consists of several production teams which were the basic collective operation and account units in rural areas.

9 It was a letter written on 7 May 1966 by Mao Zedong to Lin Biao.

10 Deng Xiaoping was then Vice-Chairman of the CPC Central Committee, Vice-Premier of the State Council and Chief of General Staff of the People's Liberation Army.

11 Jiang Qing was a member of the Politburo of the CPC Central Committee.
12 The Gang of Four includes Wang Hongwen who was Vice-Chairman of the CPC Central Committee, Zhang Chunqiao who was member of the Politburo Standing Committee of the CPC Central Committee and Vice-Premier of the State Council, Jiang Qing, and Yao Wenyuan who was member of the Politburo of the CPC Central Committee.
13 Zhou Enlai died on 8 January 1976. Qingming Day which is usually on 5 April is traditionally the time to commemorate and pay respect to the dead.
14 Yuan Baohua was then Deputy Director of the State Economic Commission.
15 Lin Hujia was then Secretary of the CPC Shanghai Committee and member of the CPC Central Committee.
16 Li Yimeng was then Deputy Director of the International Liaison Department of the CPC Central Committee.
17 Duan Yun was then Deputy Director of the State Planning Commission.
18 Hu Yaobang was then Vice-President of the Party School of the CPC Central Committee, Director of the Organization Department of the CPC Central Committee and member of the CPC Central Committee.
19 Wang Dongxing was Vice-Chairman of the CPC Central Committee, First Vice-President of the Party School of the CPC Central Committee, Director of the General Office of the CPC Central Committee and Director of its Security Bureau. He was in charge of ideological work. He arranged the arrest of the Gang of Four, under instructions of Hua Guofeng and Marshal Ye Jianying, who was Vice-Chairman of the CPC Central Committee and Vice-Chairman of the CPC Central Military Committee.
20 The prisoner's dilemma describes the situation in which everyone takes the strategy that maximizes self-interest individually, but everyone is worse off than otherwise.
21 Hainan was then under the jurisdiction of Guangdong Province.
22 Purchasing power parity (PPP) sets the ratio between the currencies of two countries at which each currency when exchanged for the other will purchase the same quantity of goods as it purchases at home excluding customs duties and costs of transport.

References

Abramovitz, Moses. 1986. "Catching up, forging ahead, and falling behind." *The Journal of Economic History* 46 (2): 385–406.
Balassa, Bela. 1970. "The economic reform in Hungary." *Economica* 37 (145): 1–22.
Bi, Jiyao, Anyuan Zhang, Changying Chen, and Yi Zhang. 2013. *The exchange rate of Renminbi: history, present and future*. Beijing: People's Publishing House.
Cai, Fang, Albert Park, and Yaohui Zhao. 2008. "The Chinese labor market in the reform era." In *China's great economic transformation*, edited by Loren Brandt and Thomas G. Rawski, 167–214. Cambridge: Cambridge University Press.
Central Committee of the Communist Party of China. 1977. *Compiled documents of the Eleventh National Congress of the Communist Party of China*, edited by Central Committee of the Communist Party of China. Beijing: People's Publishing House.
Chen, Jinhua. 2005. *The eventful years: memoirs of Chen Jinhua*. Beijing: The CPC Party History Publishing House.

Chen, Kangsheng. 1998. "Vigorously promote the development of rural economy by implementing share-holding cooperative system in an all-round way: a survey of the rural share-holding cooperative system in Huazhou City." *Southern Journal* (3): 19–20.

Chen, Xi. 1999. "156 projects and the modernization of China's industry." *Party Literature* (5): 28–34.

Chen, Xiao, Guangchun Chang, and Jiyong Yuan. 2019. "The beginning and end of the all-round contract in Dongming, Shandong." *China Archives* 543 (1): 88–89.

Chinese Society of Agricultural Machinery. 1978. *Investigation of agricultural mechanization in the United States and Canada.* Beijing: People's Publishing House.

Chow, Gregory C. 1997. "Challenges of China's economic system for economic theory." *The American Economic Review* 87 (2): 321–327.

Chuang, Yih-Chyi, and Pi-Fum Hsu. 2004. "FDI, trade, and spillover efficiency: evidence from China's manufacturing sector." *Applied Economics* 36 (10): 1103–1115.

Deng, Buren. 1995. "Assessment of political achievements must adhere to the criterion of improving economic efficiency." *Reform and Theory* (5): 12–13.

Deng, Xiaoping. 1983. "Two whatevers do not conform to Marxism." In *Selected works of Deng Xiaoping*, 38–39. Beijing: People's Press.

Du, Runsheng. 2000. "Fixing output quotas to households: a system innovation from farmers." *Hundred Year Tide* (2): 4–8.

Feng, Hui. 2007. "Mao Zedong and the second Zhengzhou conference." *Party Literature* (1): 44–51.

Feng, Wang, Yong Cai, and Baochang Gu. 2013. "Population, policy, and politics: how will history judge China's one-child policy?" *Population and Development Review* 38: 115–129.

Feng, Wang, Baochang Gu, and Yong Cai. 2016. "The end of China's one-child policy." *Studies in Family Planning* 47 (1): 83–86.

Gabriele, Alberto. 2010. "The role of the state in China's industrial development: a reassessment." *Comparative Economic Studies* 52 (3): 325–350.

Gerschenkron, Alexander. 1962. *Economic backwardness in historical perspective: a book of essays.* Cambridge, MA: Belknap Press of Harvard University Press.

Gong, Huanwen. 2016. *Notes of investigating agricultural machinery in the United States in 1976.* Shijiazhuang: Hebei Education Press.

Han, Gang. 2009. "Wan Li: how did rural reform come about?" *Lingdao Wencui* (14): 54–55.

Han, Gang. 2011. "Several historical facts about Hua Guofeng." *Yanhuangchunqiu* 26 (3): 9–18.

Hu, Albert G.Z., Gary H. Jefferson, and Qian Jinchang. 2005. "R&D and technology transfer: firm-level evidence from Chinese industry." *Review of Economics and Statistics* 87 (4): 780–786.

Hu, Angang. 2008. "Why current theories have difficulties to explain China Miracle." *People's Tribune* (4): 14–16.

Hu, Angang. 2011. "The profound connotation of the socialist system with Chinese characteristics – where China's system advantage is." *People's Tribune* (14): 23–24.

Huang, Yasheng. 2008. *Capitalism with Chinese characteristics: entrepreneurship and the state*. Cambridge: Cambridge University Press.

Jefferson, Gary H., and Jian Su. 2006. "Privatization and restructuring in China: evidence from shareholding ownership, 1995–2001." *Journal of Comparative Economics* 34 (1): 146–166.

Lee, Hong Yung. 2000. "Xiagang, the Chinese style of laying off workers." *Asian Survey* 40 (6): 914–937.

Leng, Rong, and Zuoling Wang. 2004. *Chronology of Deng Xiaoping 1975–1997.* Vol. 2. Beijing: Central Party Literature Publisher.

Li, Baihao, Xiutao Peng, and Li Huang. 2006. "A historical study on urban planning of modern emerging industries in China – focusing on the 156 key projects aided by the Soviet Union." *Urban Planning Forum* (4): 84–92.

Li, Kezhou, Baoguang Hong, Jin Wu, and Huanfeng Xu. 2008. "1976: Assigning production to household thundered in Hainai 'Xiaogang village'." *Hainan Daily*, 3 November 2008.

Li, Zhenghua. 2010. "An investigation of the 1978 State Council Plan Discussion Conference." *Contemporary China History Studies* (2): 4–13.

Lin, Yifu. 2008. "Current theories still have difficulties to explain China Miracle." *People's Tribune* (4): 14–15.

Lin, Yifu. 2016. "It is not feasible to copy the western mainstream economic theory." *Qiushi* (20): 57–59.

Lin, Yifu. 2017. "Sticking to the doctrine of 'taking sutras from the west' is very harmful." *Lilun Daobao* (8): 11.

Lin, Justin Yifu. 2013. "Demystifying the Chinese economy." *Australian Economic Review* 46 (3): 259–268.

Lin, Justin Yifu, Fang Cai, and Zhou Li. 2003. *The China miracle: development strategy and economic reform*. Revised ed. Hong Kong: Chinese University Press.

Liu, Jintian. 2018. "Record of Deng Xiaoping's visit to Japan in 1978." *Across Time and Space* (10): 4–9.

Liu, Yan. 2014. "Overseas investigation by senior leaders at the beginning of Reform and Opening." *Literary Circles of CPC History* (19): 37–43.

Liu, Yuhua. 2009. "Xiaogang village: the first village of China's rural reform." *Director of Village Committee* (9): 32.

Liu, Zhonghua, and Baohong Xie. 2000. "On issues related to affiliation." *Journal of Southwest University of Political Science and Law* 2 (2): 81–83.

Ma, Shexiang. 2009. "Retrospect and reflection on the pilot project of contracting production to households in Xiaojingzhuang, Shannan district: an interview with Zhou Yueli." *Journal of Chinese Communist Party History Studies* (4): 103–106.

Murphy, Kevin M., Andrei Shleifer, and Robert W. Vishny. 1992. "The transition to a market economy: pitfalls of partial reform." *The Quarterly Journal of Economics* 107 (3): 889–906.

National Bureau of Statistics of China. 1979. *1978 statistical bulletin on national economic and social development*, edited by National Bureau of Statistics of China. Beijing.

National Bureau of Statistics of China. 1980. *1979 statistical bulletin on national economic and social development*, edited by National Bureau of Statistics of China. Beijing.

National Bureau of Statistics of China. 1981. *1980 statistical bulletin on national economic and social development*, edited by National Bureau of Statistics of China. Beijing.

National Bureau of Statistics of China. 1982. *1981 statistical bulletin on national economic and social development*, edited by National Bureau of Statistics of China. Beijing.

National Bureau of Statistics of China. 1985. *1984 statistical bulletin on national economic and social development*, edited by National Bureau of Statistics of China. Beijing.

Ni, Degang. 2014. "Review Comrade Deng Xiaoping's political advice – commemorating the 110 anniversary of the birth of Comrade Deng Xiaoping." *The Science of Leadership Forum* (9): 56–57.

Nolan, Peter, and Xiaoqiang Wang. 1999. "Beyond privatization: institutional innovation and growth in China's large state-owned enterprises." *World Development* 27 (1): 169–200.

Pan, Fei. 2018. "Unveiling: Wan Li and rural reform in Anhui." *Across Time and Space* (11): 8–15.

Pan, Hong. 2010. "Complete and accurate understanding of Deng Xiaoping's important 16 September talk." *Bridge of Century* (3): 16–18.

Pan, Zhaodong. 2008. "Talking about Zhao Chounv's contracting event." *China's Ethnic Groups* (5): 52–53.

Party Literature Research Center of the CPC Central Committee. 1989. *Comrade Deng Xiaoping on adhering to four cardinal principles and combating bourgeois liberalization*. Beijing: People's Publishing House.

Party Literature Research Center of the CPC Central Committee. 2005. "Before and after crossing the price pass in 1988." *Yanhuangchunqiu* (10): 22–25.

Quan, Heng. 2004. "All-round development and innovation of cadre assessment system." *Digest of Party and Government Cadres* (1): 25–26.

Ramo, Joshua Cooper. 2004. *The Beijing consensus*. London: Foreign Policy Centre

Sapir, Andre. 1980. "Economic growth and factor substitution: what happened to the Yugoslav miracle?" *The Economic Journal* 90 (358): 294–313.

Schoenhals, Michael. 1991. "The 1978 truth criterion controversy." *The China Quarterly* 126: 243–268.

Schroeder, Gertrude E. 1990. "Economic reform of socialism: the Soviet record." *The Annals of the American Academy of Political and Social Science* 507 (1): 35–43.

Sheng, Hong. 2012. "The nature, performance and reform of state owned enterprises." *China Non-governmental Science Technology and Economy* (6): 36–41.

Sheng, Hong, Nong Zhao, Junfeng Yang, Pu Qian, Jianqiang Guan, and Xiaojing Yang. 2011. *The nature, performance and reform of state owned enterprises*. Beijing: Unirule Institute of Economics.

Summers, Lawrence H., and Vinod Thomas. 1993. "Recent lessons of development." *The World Bank Research Observer* 8 (2): 241–254.

Sun, Xuewen. 1999. "Reform and progress of national economy in macro-adjustment and control – implementation of the new eight character guiding principles of adjustment, reform, consolidation and improvement." *Materials from CPC History* (9): 2–6.

Tang, Rimei. 2004. "On the status of 156 projects in China's initial industrialization." *Theory Horizon* 1: 39.

Van Reenen, John, and Linda Yueh. 2012. "Why has China grown so fast? The role of international technology transfer." In *Centre for economic performance discussion papers*, edited by Oxford University. Oxford.

Wang, Shuguang. 2017. *Rural China*. Beijing: Peking University Press.

Wang, Shuo. 2006. "The establishment of Shenzhen special economic zone (1979–1986)." *Researches in Chinese Economic History* (3): 36–44.

Wang, Tao. 2014. "1979 theoretical work discussion conference." *Literary Circles of CPC History* (13): 36–42.

Wang, Tao, Xiuzhen Li, and Xiangyang Liang. 2004. "Note of a visit to Wu Tangsheng, the pioneer of contracting production to households." *Hongguangjiao* (5): 25–27.

Wang, Wenxiang. 1986. *China's special economic zones and fourteen opening cities*. Beijing: China Prospect Publishing House.

Williamson, John. 2000. "What should the World Bank think about the Washington Consensus?" *The World Bank Research Observer* 15 (2): 251–264.

Williamson, John. 2004. "The strange history of the Washington consensus." *Journal of Post Keynesian Economics* 27 (2): 195–206.

Williamson, John. 2012. "Is the 'Beijing consensus' now dominant?" *Asia Policy* (13): 1–16.

Wu, Dayan, and Diankeng Huang. 1996. "Rural affiliated firms need to be normalized urgently." *People's Procuratorate* (7): 51–53.

Wu, Xiang. 1996. "The first step of China's rural reform – reading the part on Anhui rural reform of the selected works of Wan Li." *Journal of Chinese Communist Party History Studies* (3): 11–16.

Xiang, Nan. 1979. "Agricultural mechanization in our country must be realized – talking about the current situation of agricultural mechanization in Europe and America." *Farm Machinery* (1): 2–7.

Xiao, Lijian. 2016. *China's capital market: development path and risk control*. Beijing: China Financial and Economic Publishing House.

Xie, Duyang. 1983. "How has the past four years passed? – a brief review on the formulation and implementation of the guiding principle of adjustment, reform, consolidation and improvement." *Macroeconomics* (33): 2–11.

Xin, Ziling. 2008. "The historical change in the understanding of the bourgeoisies." *Yanhuangchunqiu* (3): 15–21.

Xu, Lianfang. 1994. "Development situation and countermeasure of rural joint-stock cooperative system in our province." *Academic Review* (12): 54–56.

Yang, Jisheng. 2009. "Price reform: a risky step in economic reform." *Yanhuangchunqiu* (3): 18–23.

Yu, Guangyuan. 1998a. "Recollection of the Central Committee Work Conference before the Third Plenum of the Eleventh Central Committee (part 2): thirty-six days that changed China's historical course." *Hundred Year Tide* (6): 4–19.

Yu, Guangyuan. 1998b. "Thirty-six days that changed China's historical course." *Hundred Year Tide* (5): 4–14.

Yuan, Xiaojiang. 2017. "Gu Mu led a delegation to investigate five European countries in 1978." *Hundred Year Tide* (10): 13–22.

Zhang, Han, Xin Zhang, and Yanyan Shi. 2008. "The village that divided farmland to groups earliest." *Party Building* (7): 45–46.

Zhang, Jiaobang. 1999. "An investigation of affiliation type private enterprises in the Pearl River Delta." *South China Economy* (5): 53–55.

Zhang, Qing, and Bruce Felmingham. 2002. "The role of FDI, exports and spillover effects in the regional development of China." *Journal of Development Studies* 38 (4): 157–178.

Zhang, Shaochun. 2010. "An investigation of Li Xiannian and the 'don't do much ado about nothing' principle." *Contemporary China History Studies* (5): 90–93.

Zhang, Shujun. 1998. *A great change – records of the Third Plenum of the Eleventh Central Committee of the Communist Party of China.* Hangzhou: Zhejiang People's Publishing House.

Zhang, Weiwei. 2006. "The allure of the Chinese model." *International Herald Tribune* 2.

Zhu, Erpei. 1995. *Chronicle of Baosteel.* Shanghai: Shanghai Academy of Social Science Press.

Zhu, Liang. 2008. "The Tito-Hua Guofeng exchange of visits – the activities in foreign affairs that brought inspirations to the reform and opening." *Yanhuangchunqiu* (8): 8–10.

2 Interest rate control and China's economic growth

Economic growth is the growth of output. Output is determined by production factors which include labour (workers), capital (equipment etc.) and technology that is subsumed in the sophistication of equipment and the expertise of labour force. For a certain technological level, the output is determined primarily by labour and capital inputs. Borrowing Thomas Kuhn's terminology for scientific progress (Kuhn 1962), we might classify economic growth into two types: paradigm-changing growth and normal growth. Paradigm-changing growth occurs when an economy's dominant production technologies are replaced or shifted by new technologies, such as industrialization of an agricultural country. For a country during its paradigm-changing growth stage, high saving rates and high investment rates will result in high growth rates. Normal growth happens when there is no fundamental change in the economy's dominant production technologies, such as the economic growth of developed countries since 1970. The normal growth relies on small incremental process innovations and product innovations. High saving rates and high investment rates during the normal growth stage may lead to dynamic inefficiency, which means that further increasing capital stock will reduce the overall utility of current and future generations.

Some economists, especially some of those who advocate the China Model, fail to understand the difference between paradigm-changing growth and normal growth. They compare China's rapid growth with Russia's shock therapy–caused economic contraction to show that China's gradualist dual-track system is the correct approach for reform. They might think that Russia could have achieved similar rapid growth had it used China's approach. However, the two countries are not comparable in their transition from a planned economy to a market economy. While China was still to be industrialized in 1978 with 82.1% of its population living in rural areas, Russia had completed its industrialization with 31.3% of its population in rural areas. According to Maddison's database (Bolt et al. 2018) and World Bank data, Russia's real GDP per capita in 2011 constant international dollars was $19,098 (and the former Soviet Union's was $14,099) in 1978 and in comparison the second largest capitalist developed economy Japan's was $19,804; after 38 years of annual 9.5% phenomenal growth, China's was $12,569 in 2016 and its rural population was 43.26%. The Soviet economy stagnated in 1970s because it was approaching its normal growth under the central planning system. In contrast, China's economy had grown strongly by 1978 whenever its economy was not disrupted by the political movements and unrealistic economic campaigns such as the Great Leap Forward (1958–1960) launched by Mao Zedong and the CPC Central Committee (Borensztein and Ostry 1996).

Since a country's living standard depends on its output per capita which is more related to capital stock per unit labour, the growth of capital stock is essential for a country's economic growth before reaching its normal growth. China had the largest rural population in the world when its reform and opening started in 1978, but as a developing country, China's capital stock was very low so that it had to make more investment to increase its capital stock. Capital and investment ultimately come from national saving, the part of national income that is not used for consumption. China has maintained very high national saving rates over the past four decades, which has been an essential factor that drives China's rapid economic growth.

How has China managed to have an increasingly high saving rate over the three decades from 1978 to 2008 and to maintain it close to 50% in the past ten years? The monetary policy of China's central bank partly contributes to it. This chapter will first look at the possible relationship between China's rapid economic growth and its high saving rates in Section 2.1; then examine its central bank's policy on interest rates since 1978 in Section 2.2; introduce a growth model with interest rate control in Section 2.3; investigate the impact of below-equilibrium interest rates in Section 2.4; discuss the implications of this model in Section 2.5; and summarize in Section 2.6.

2.1 China's growth rates and saving rates

According to the Solow-Swan growth model (Solow 1956; Swan 1956), before an economy reaches its steady state within the constraints of contemporary production technologies, its saving rate is the key determinant of its growth rate (see Appendix 2.A for a brief introduction of the model). The higher the saving rate, the faster the growth. Once the economy has reached its steady state, without technological progress to raise the level of its steady state, its output per unit labour will no longer grow. Before 1978, China with GDP per capita at just over US$300 (in constant 2010 US$) was far from reaching its steady state, compared either with that of the Soviet Union under the central planning system or with that of the US under the market system. Therefore, its saving rate should have played an important role in its subsequent economic growth.

An earlier model, the Harold-Domar model, considers the saving rate or equivalently the investment rate being the driving force of economic growth (Harrod 1939; Domar 1946). When the marginal product of capital (MPK)[1] is constant, the economic growth rate g is a function of the saving rate s for any given levels of output and capital stock,

$$g = \frac{\Delta Y}{Y} = s\frac{Y}{K} - \delta \tag{2.1}$$

In the above equation, Y is the output, K the capital stock, and δ the depreciation rate of the capital stock. According to this model, a high saving rate might be one of the key factors underlying the fast growth of China's economy.

To understand whether China has had high saving rates which might underlie China's rapid growth, we compare China with India in terms of their saving and growth rates in the past four decades. The two countries had similar populations and at similar stages of development in the late 1970s. In 1978 India's GDP per capita was US$437.8, while China's US$307.1 (in constant 2010 US$). The growth rates and saving rates of the two countries are shown in Figure 2.1. In the period 1978–2018, China's economy generally grows faster than India's, and remarkably China's gross saving[2] rate has been consistently much higher than India's.

Using the Harold-Domar model, we may conclude that the gross saving rate is the key factor that underlies the difference in the GDP growth rate between China and India. India's population growth during this period is faster than China's, which could affect the growth of its capital stock per person and consequently GDP per capita. If China and India have a similar level of the MPK and depreciation rate of capital stock, China's higher saving rate has not generated a proportionally higher growth rate than India's. Using the Solow-Swan model, we can understand why although China's saving rate continues to be much higher than India's, the difference in growth rates between the two countries becomes smaller since 2010. It is because China is closer than India to its steady state with the current production technologies.

Since incremental innovations occur all the time, Solow's steady state is a theoretical construction which does not exist in the real world in its pure form. The steady state in the real world actually is the normal growth we described earlier. It depends on incremental process innovations[3] and product innovations[4] rather than high saving rates and high investment rates. The difference in the level of net saving[5] rates between paradigm-changing

(A)

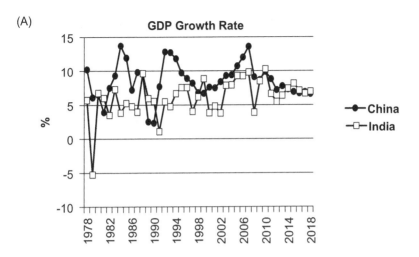

(B)

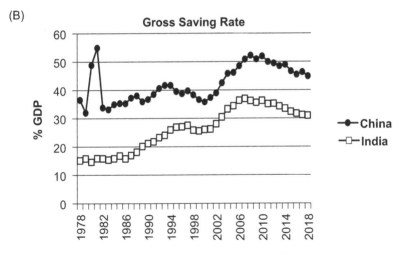

Figure 2.1 GDP growth rates and the gross saving rates of China and India

*Sourc*e: World Bank.

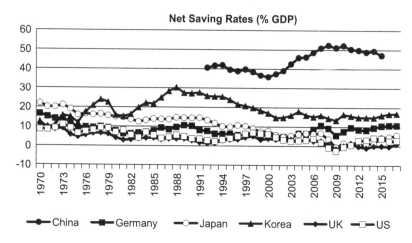

Figure 2.2 Net saving rates of China, Germany, Japan, Korea, the UK and the US. China's data are between 1992 and 2015 and others' between 1970 and 2017

Source: OECD.

growth economies and normal growth economies is more remarkable. The gross savings of paradigm-changing economies such as China are mainly net savings used to increase their capital stock, whereas the net saving rates of normal growth economies such as the US and the UK are low because their gross savings are mainly used to replace depreciated capital stock. Figure 2.2 shows the net saving rates of China, Korea and several developed countries, according to data from the Organisation of Economic Cooperation and Development (OECD).

The UK and the US are the earliest to be industrialized and their net saving rates have been below 10% since 1970. Japan was industrialized later and its net saving rate drops from over 20% in the early 1970s to below 10% since the late 1990s. The newly industrialized Korea decreased from over 20% in the 1980s to below 20% since the mid-1990s. Korea's GDP per capita (in constant 2011 international dollar) reached $15,760 in 1994, which is at the similar level of Japan's in 1970 at $15,286. Germany's net saving rate usually includes a huge current account surplus and net capital outflow, such that its net domestic investment rate is low; its current account surplus was 8.9% of GDP in 2015. When an economy has completed its paradigm change (from an agricultural economy to an industrial economy), high saving rates will no longer be effective in producing fast growth before its next paradigm-change stage. Therefore, most high-income industrialized countries have low net saving rates. Since China has been in its paradigm-changing growth so far, its high saving rates result in its rapid growth.

2.2 Interest rate control in China

China's rapid economic growth may be explained by its high saving rates. One of the key features in China's monetary policies is interest rate control, which keeps interest rates well below the market equilibrium level. Cutting interest rates has been an important tool for central banks in developed countries to stimulate economic growth. Persistent low interest rates might be an essential cause of China's high saving rate. China's financial industry is strictly regulated and largely controlled by the government, and the implementation of interest rate control has been an evolving process. From 1950 to 1979, the PBOC was the only bank in the PRC, as other banks within mainland China were actually either organized as divisions of the PBOC or non-deposit-taking agencies. In the era of the planned economy, financial resources were allocated by government plans, and all interest rates were set by the government through the PBOC. Households were encouraged to save and deposit their savings at branches of the PBOC and (for farmers) Rural Credit Cooperatives.

With increased emphasis on economic construction after October 1976, it was recognized that the banking system should play a more important role in the economy. On 28 November 1977, the State Council issued *Several Provisions on Rectifying and Strengthening Bank Work*, which raised the PBOC to the ministry level under the State Council and separated the PBOC from the Ministry of Finance. The First Meeting of the Fifth National People's Congress formally approved the ministry status of the PBOC in March 1978. ABC re-formed as an independent specialized bank in February 1979 to support economic growth in rural areas, and BOC became an independent specialized bank on 13 March 1979. CCB gained independence from the Ministry of Finance in August 1979. The PBOC was still responsible for both central banking and commercial banking operations before it began to function exclusively as a central bank on 1 January 1984. It then transferred its commercial banking operations to the newly created ICBC. The PBOC has a dual mandate of stabilizing the currency and maintaining robust growth; it also has an acknowledged but implicit mandate to maintain financial stability (Bell and Feng 2013).

The establishment of specialized banks brought about the issue of whether to use the surplus fund of one bank to bridge temporary funding gap in another bank. The PBOC issued on 8 October 1984 the *Proposed Regulations of Credit Fund Management* to be implemented on 1 January 1985, which approved lending between specialized state-owned banks. Local interbank lending platforms were formed in many cities, with rates negotiated between counterparties. The *Provisional Regulations of the People's Republic of China on the Control of Banks* promulgated by the State Council on 7 January 1986 permitted interbank lending and allowed the state-owned specialized banks to operate deposits, loans, settlement of accounts and personal savings deposits in national and foreign currencies. It also allowed joint-stock and city commercial banks to be set up by central government, local governments and firms.

The Provisional Regulations gave the PBOC the authority to decree the deposit rate cap (the highest deposit rate) and the lending rate floor (the lowest lending rate) and to set the range of interest rates allowed to vary by the state-owned formerly specialized banks and joint-stock or city commercial banks. In 1993, the PBOC set the ceiling and the floor for lending rates at 20% above and 10% below the benchmark rates. The ceiling for lending rates was reduced to 10% above the benchmark rates in 1996, increased to 20% above in 1998 for loans to small enterprises, increased to 30% above for loans made by financial institutions at the county level or below in 1999, increased to 70% above on 1 January 2004, and was removed on 29 October 2004. The floor for lending rates was reduced from 10% below benchmark rates to 20% below on 7 June 2012, reduced to 30% below on 5 July 2012, and removed on 20 July 2013 (China Statistical Yearbooks). For residential mortgage lending, special measures apply.

The PBOC tends to have a stricter control over the deposit rates. The deposit rates were allowed to float downward to a floor of 10% below the benchmark deposit rates on 29 October 2004, and they were allowed to float upward to a ceiling of 10% above the benchmark rates on 7 June 2012. The ceiling for deposit rates was increased to 20% above on 22 November 2014, to 30% above on 1 March 2015, to 50% above on 11 May 2015, removed for deposits with two-year and three-year fixed terms on 27 August 2015, and removed for all deposits on 23 October 2015. The PBOC continues to issue benchmark rates for lending and deposits. These benchmark rates and ceilings are the most powerful instrument to affect market interest rates and bank lending rates, and they help to anchor the whole interest rates system (He and Wang 2012; He, Wang, and Yu 2015). The PBOC implicitly shapes the term structure by imposing ceilings on deposit rates of different maturities. Deposits are the main funding source for commercial banks, which dominate the Chinese financial system. Interest rates used internally by banks for capital budgeting and transfer pricing are still based on benchmark deposit rates instead of market rates such as repo rates (Jiang 2012).

While state-owned specialized banks and commercial banks must follow the PBOC decreed rates, individuals and non-banking institutions are not allowed to raise funds by taking deposits. Besides decreeing deposit rates and lending rates for commercial banks and other institutions, the PBOC also sets interest rates for its operations: 1) lending rates of refinance facilities such as central bank relending rates and rediscount rates, 2) deposit rates for required reserves and excess reserves. 3) open-market operation rates such as central bank repo rates and central bank bill rates, which have become increasingly important tools to signal the PBOC's policy intentions and to guide market interest rates toward desired levels (Zhang 2012).

Apart from the administered deposit and lending rates, there are market-determined interest rates, but administered interest rates are still key determinants of both the level and volatility of the market determined rates (He, Wang, and Yu 2015). After long preparation, the PBOC established a unified interbank trading platform in Shanghai on 3 January 1996. The China Interbank Offered Rates (CHIBORs) is based on the activities on this platform. The interbank repo market introduced on 6 June 1997 soon replaced the interbank loan market to become the major source of short-term liquidity for banks, resulting in the compilation of repo fixing rates initially for overnight, 7-day and 14-day tenors, which became a widely used benchmark in the interbank market. The PBOC influences this market via open market operations. The relatively short maturity in repo transactions has restrained interbank funding with longer tenors. In order to build a benchmark yield curve, the PBOC established the Shanghai Interbank Offered Rates (SHIBORs) on 4 January 2007, which is set in a similar way to the London Interbank Offered Rate (LIBOR), with rates calculated as the arithmetic average of the Chinese currency RMB offered rates by the participating banks.

The SHIBORs have not only increased turnover in the interbank loan market, but also facilitated the pricing of a range of interest rate derivatives. However, a large portion of interbank transactions are concentrated at short tenors of one month or less; for example, more than half of the trading days registered no transactions for lending of six months to one year in the repo and interbank loan markets during the period 2010 to 2013. This uneven distribution has restrained use of the money-market rates as the benchmark for pricing loans with longer maturities. It is found that short-term interbank lending rates are not able to act as an independent benchmark for asset pricing, or an independent indicator of macroeconomic or financial conditions (Porter and Xu 2013; He, Wang, and Yu 2015).

There has been large difference between the rate of return to capital in China, which is estimated at around 20% (Bai, Hsieh, and Qian 2006), and the deposit and lending rates decreed by the PBOC for most time since 1978 (Lardy 2008; Porter and Xu 2013; He, Wang, and Yu 2015). Interest rates are kept at artificially low levels to extract transfers or subsidies from households to the corporate sector, particularly the SOEs (Lardy 2008). As the deposit rate ceilings are persistently below their equilibrium level, the PBOC must rely on quantity-based instruments such as aggregate credit quotas and reserve requirement ratios to maintain financial stability. The PBOC also uses "unconventional" instruments, like the "window guidance" (giving instructions to the commercial banks on their credit activity) and selective credit controls (for particular sectors) which are also called qualitative instruments (Goodfriend and Prasad 2006).

2.3 A growth through interest rate control model

In this and the following sections, I will present a growth through interest rate control model developed in an earlier study to explain China's high saving rate and high growth rate (Ma 2017). This growth model considers a simplified scenario in order to catch the key underlying causes and processes of China's rapid economic growth. There are two economies in this model: the domestic economy and the foreign economy, which are in paradigm-changing growth and normal growth, respectively. The foreign economy is more developed than the domestic economy; therefore, foreign economy has the comparative advantage[6] in capital intensive and technology intensive sectors, while the domestic economy has the comparative advantage in labour intensive and traditional industrial sectors. There are four types of economic agent or player in this model: domestic workers, domestic firms, the central bank and the foreign countries. Markets are where agents in the same economy or different economies interact. There are six types of market: the domestic commodity and service market, the international commodity and service market, the domestic labour market, the domestic financial market, the international financial market, and the foreign exchange market (see Appendix 2.B for a detailed description).

2.3.1 The economic agents

New workers come from the labour force pool in the rural area and the labour supply level depends on the wage rate. Their objective is to maximize their expected lifetime utility. The labour supply curve slopes upwards. The workers are precautionary or buffer-stock savers (Skinner 1988; Zeldes 1989; Deaton 1991; Carroll, Hall, and Zeldes 1992; Carroll 1997; Carroll and Samwick 1998), because of the uncertainty in their future income and the economy. Carroll shows that these buffer-stock models imply that consumers will have a target wealth-to-income ratio such that if wealth is below the target, income will exceed consumption and wealth will rise (Carroll, Hall, and Zeldes 1992; Carroll 1997). It has been estimated that 45% of total net worth, half of non-housing, non-business wealth, and about one-third of very liquid assets of households younger than age 50 are held as a precaution against the systematically greater uncertainty that some households face as compared with others (Carroll and Samwick 1998). Compared with developed countries, the social security system in China is not well established, so that workers face more uncertainty in terms of their future income and standard of living. An important part of China's reform in its first 20 to 30 years was to remove social welfare and job security, figuratively called "big pot meal" and "iron rice bowl" in China, which were enjoyed by SOE and UCOE employees before 1978. Researches on the saving rates of Chinese households also indicate marked precautionary saving behaviours (Ma and Yi 2010; Song and Yang 2010; Chamon and Prasad 2010; Chamon, Liu, and Prasad 2013).

Since 1978, a large proportion of the labour force in China are migrant workers from rural areas who face greater uncertainty in their future income and enjoy little social welfare compared with workers with urban residence register (hukou). The declining public provision of education, health and housing services as well as more market mechanism in wage determination for workers with urban residence register also increased uncertainty in their overall incomes and standard of living. Consequently both workers with rural and urban residence registers behave as precautionary/buffer-stock savers and save to reach their wealth target. For precautionary/buffer-stock savers, before reaching their saving target, they will increase their saving rates when their incomes increase, which has been confirmed by empirical studies on Chinese household surveys (Chamon, Liu, and Prasad 2013; Chamon and Prasad 2010; Song and Yang 2010). A lower interest rate might also increase their optimal saving rate, because a lower interest rate would slow down their pace to reach their wealth targets if they do not increase their saving rates.

In a world with certainty or certainty equivalence,[7] the workers become life-cycle savers who save a certain percentages of their incomes before retirement for post-retirement consumption (Modigliani 1986). The life-cycle model with certainty equivalence has been popular for investigating people's consumption and saving behaviours. It predicts a hump-shape age-wealth profile for workers who save during their working ages and dissave during retirement. However, Kotlikoff and Summers find little hump-saving in the US, and there are also other empirical studies which do not support the life-cycle model (Kotlikoff and Summers 1981). The life-cycle model is still useful as a benchmark for predicting people's saving behaviour, while uncertainty will increase people's saving rate (Skinner 1988; Zeldes 1989; Deaton 1991; Carroll 1997; Carroll and Samwick 1998).

The firms organize production activities in the economy, pay workers for their labour, sell goods to workers and foreign countries and exchange foreign currencies for home currency with the central bank. The objective of a firm is to maximize its net present value which is a function of its discounted future profits. For simplicity, we assume that the domestic economy has the same production function with its arguments as capital stock and labour force employed in the economy, and all profits of the firms are part of the national savings. This assumption ignores the facts that SOEs and UCOEs need to pay taxes to the government, SOEs may hand certain proportions of their profits to the government and the owners of the private enterprises may consume part of their firms' profits, because these are relatively small compared with the GDP and their omission helps find out the key mechanisms and relationships.

Since 1978, thousands of private enterprises have emerged, most state-owned and collectively owned firms have been privatized. The remaining SOEs are big companies many of which are listed companies with shares traded at the stock market. The private enterprises have expanded rapidly in the past 30 years because their MPKs are much higher than banks' lending rates so that firms invest as much as they can. The consumption by the owners of private enterprises is only a tiny fraction of their profits during the period of rapid expansion. The SOEs did not turn over their profits to the state between 1994 and 2007 and they hand only a small fraction of their profits to the state from 2008. The assumption that all firms' profits belong to the national savings tries to catch these key features of firms in China since 1978.

To simplify the model, we use the central bank to represent the banking system and assume that it is a costless intermediary which decrees the deposit rate and the lending rate, manages the foreign exchanges and holds foreign bonds. The central bank takes deposits from the workers and makes loans to the firms. The objective of the central bank is to maximize the GDP. The specification here tries to abstract some key features of the banking system in China. The PBOC has maintaining robust growth as part of its mandate, and it probably has greater influence on the commercial banks, and thus on the formal credit market than its Western counterparts. For most time since 1978, the banks have a dominant role in the Chinese financial market and their main business has been to take deposits from the savers and lend to the borrowers. They had to use interest rates within the range decreed by the PBOC (Bell and Feng 2013).

The foreign countries buy goods from the firms in the domestic economy by paying foreign currencies and sell bonds to (i.e. borrow money from) the central bank of the domestic economy by paying the international interest rate. The foreign countries' demand for goods from the domestic economy depends on the price level of the exported goods relative to the price level of the foreign countries. When the price of the exported goods is increasing, the demand for those goods is generally decreasing. The central bank buys foreign bonds to earn returns on the foreign exchange reserves it holds. The purchase of goods by foreign countries creates pressure on the domestic currency to appreciate and appreciation of the domestic currency reduces the competitiveness of the goods produced by the domestic firms. The objective of the foreign countries is to maximize the total utility of their residents.

2.3.2 The markets

In the domestic commodity and service market, the firms buy commodities and services for investment, while the workers buy them for consumption. On the international commodity and service market, the firms sell their products and services to foreign countries and buy goods and technologies from foreign countries for capital investment. The firms may also buy consumption goods from foreign countries and resell them to domestic workers. On the international commodity and service market, the demand from foreign countries is determined by three factors: 1) the price difference between the two economies; 2) differentiation between products of the two economies; 3) familiarity with the imported goods.

The supply by the domestic economy to the international commodity and service market depends on the price difference between the international market price and the domestic price, trade and economic policies in the domestic economy, and the domestic demand and GDP. The GDP of the foreign economy is divided into two components: tradable goods and services and non-tradable goods and services.[8] The exports of the domestic economy are substitutes of the tradable goods and services in the foreign economy. The tradable goods and services can be further divided into two categories: the tradable goods for which the domestic economy has the comparative advantage and the tradable goods for which the domestic economy has no comparative advantage. With technological progress, the share in the (foreign) GDP of tradable goods in the traditional industries will decrease. Since the domestic economy also progresses technologically, we assume that the proportion of the traditional tradable goods in the foreign GDP, which can be replaced by exports from the domestic economy, is a relatively constant value.

The domestic labour market is where firms find their employees and workers find their jobs in industries, service sectors and commercially run agriculture firms. China used to have a large reserve labour pool in rural areas in the agriculture sector, where unemployment is implicit because all the farmers share the farming workload on the land which they have land-use right. Over 82% of the population in 1978 were agricultural rural residents (National Bureau of Statistics of China 2011), and even now the migrant workers from rural areas with agricultural residence register cannot enjoy the same social welfare benefits as the urban residents working in the same region. Farmers working on their own land are not considered to be employed as workers in this model, and they belong to the reserve labour pool. The demand for labour is determined by the output of the domestic economy, the GDP and the wage rate. The labour supply is determined by the wage rate and the reserve labour pool in rural areas. The higher the wage rate, the more the people want to become a worker. The size of labour supply and its dependence on the wage rate are influenced by the size of the reserve labour pool.

The domestic financial market is where the primary lenders provide the loanable funds and the ultimate borrowers obtain the funds for investment in the capital stock. The workers in this model are savers and the primary lenders, and the firms are (both savers/investors with their own profits and) the ultimate borrowers. The central bank is the intermediary that sets the interest rate, and for simplicity we assume that the lending rate is the same as the deposit rate. Some firms may become savers if they decide not to invest their profits. In an open economy, the equilibrium interest rate should be equal to the optimal MPK, the optimal marginal product of labour (MPL)[9] as well as the international interest rate. If the interest rate r is set at a value smaller than the current MPK, the firms will invest all its profits and borrow more funds to invest until MPK = r. The national savings include both the firms' profits and the workers' savings.

At the early stage of industrialization, the national saving rate should be higher than later stages before the first generation of workers start their retirement, because the savings for retirement are not consumed yet. If all workers are in employment for the same number of years with the same wage growth rate and the same optimal saving rate and their ages are evenly distributed, we can estimate the total savings of the workers when the first age group start their retirement (see Appendix 2.C). If the wage growth rate is zero and the number of workers is stable, when the first age group of workers start their retirement, the value of the total saving will become stable as well. As the wage growth rate (of wages per worker) is usually larger than zero, the value of total savings will grow with wages. During the industrialization, the number of workers will increase rapidly, and therefore the total savings will not become stable, even if the wage growth rate is zero and the first age group of workers have retired.

Since the workers are precautionary/buffer-stock savers rather than certainty equivalent life-cycle savers, they will save more than what the life-cycle model predicts. Before their savings reach their target wealth, the workers, especially the migrant workers from rural areas, with little personal wealth and low wage income would increase their saving rate when their wages increase or interest rate decreases. By setting the interest rate lower (than equilibrium rate), the central bank increases the national savings: firstly, the precautionary/buffer-stock saving workers might increase their saving rate in order to reach their target wealth, as lower interest rates imply slower growth of their personal wealth; secondly, firms can not only invest their own profits, but also borrow cheaply from workers' savings, which increases firms' profits (savings) and decreases workers' consumption because the workers receive less interest income. The second effect of lower interest rates plays a more important role in increasing national savings than the first effect. Consequently, the firms' savings will grow faster than the workers' savings as proportions of GDP. It has been found that as government savings and enterprises' savings both grow faster than households' savings, their proportions of savings in terms of GDP have increased substantially, while households' proportion has been largely stable. The proportion of households' savings in terms of GDP is still generally larger than those of government and enterprises (He and Cao 2007; Ma and Yi 2010).

The domestic financial market described here tries to catch the key features of the Chinese financial market during the past four decades since 1978. The deposit rates and lending rates have been controlled by the PBOC, and the entry of new firms into the financial sector has been strictly regulated by the government. There was a lack of investment instruments other than bank deposits probably until 2008. The bond market was underdeveloped and for the average households the return from investing in the Chinese stock market was even lower than the bank deposit interest rate. China's capital account is effectively closed, with tight restrictions on the access of domestic citizens to the international asset markets (Chang, Liu, and Spiegel 2015).

The international financial market is where the lenders in one country provide funds to borrowers from other countries and the borrowers in one country obtain funds from other countries. The central bank enforces control over cross-border capital flows. When there is a current account surplus in the domestic economy, the central bank will invest its foreign exchange reserves in foreign bonds to earn the international interest rate. As exporters' foreign currencies are bought by the central bank with domestic currency which it can print, the central bank will invest almost all of its foreign exchange reserves in foreign bonds. National savings in one period (year) include the part of returns from foreign assets that is not consumed. The saving can be invested in capital stock as well as in foreign assets. National savings in excess of domestic capital formation flow into net foreign asset accumulation.

The foreign exchange market is where the firms sell their foreign currencies earned from exporting their products in return for the domestic currency which can be used for labour and capital spending, and the firms buy foreign currencies with the domestic currency to pay for their imports. In this model, the central bank enforces control over foreign exchange transactions such that all sellers and buyers have to make transactions with the central bank.

As foreign demand for domestic goods and services depends on the domestic price level relative to the international market price level, the nominal exchange rate of the domestic currency becomes an important factor in determining the net exports. According to the theory of purchasing-power parity, the long-run equilibrium nominal exchange rate e^* should be equal to the ratio between domestic price P_D and the foreign price P_F, that is, $e^* = P_D/P_F$. Because of interest rate arbitrage, there should be interest rate parity. Domestic interest rate is linked to the nominal exchange rate in an open economy. By setting the domestic interest rate low, the central bank reduces the wages of workers and increases their savings, which leads to higher national savings and abundant loanable funds for the international financial market. The abundance of loanable funds helps decrease real interest rate and increase the capital outflow.

The foreign exchange market has been regulated in China through current account management, capital account management and exchange rate management. The PBOC adopted a dual-track foreign exchange rate system after 1978, and slowly moved toward a convertible (current account) system between 1979 and 1993. Firms could sell and buy foreign currencies at foreign exchange swap centres using unofficial exchange rates determined by market demand and supply. The dual-track system was abolished on 1 January 1994 and RMB current account items became conditionally convertible. The China Foreign Exchange Trade System was established on 18 April 1994 as the unified foreign exchange market with managed floating exchange rates based on market demand and supply. The RMB was essentially pegged to the US dollar until 2005, and allowed to move within narrow bands set around a base rate determined by a basket of foreign currencies from 21 July 2005. The specification in the present model catches the main features of the exchange rate control by China over the past four decades.

2.4   The market equilibriums and the economic growth

One important cause of China's rapid economic growth is the introduction of market mechanism and the adoption of advanced production technologies through high levels of investment. Market mechanism leads to optimal allocation of scarce resources in terms of return on capital. With market opening, advanced technology and global capital come into China. Economic growth is the result of dynamic equilibrium in the six markets, underlain by the interactions between the economic agents involved in those markets.

2.4.1 The equilibrium of the domestic economy

Since capital is scarcer than labour in the domestic economy at the beginning of its paradigm-changing growth stage, it is optimal for firms and entrepreneurs in a market economy to develop labour intensive business first. With the interest rate lower than the international market equilibrium rate and the corresponding MPK, the firms will invest to increase their production capacity as much as the funds available, while the workers have a higher saving rate. The investments can be classified into two categories: 1) investment in capital stocks for producing goods to be used as capital stocks and 2) investment in capital stocks for producing consumer goods. An economy during its early paradigm-changing growth is likely to invest mainly in capital stocks for producing consumer goods, because the domestic economy during that stage lacks the capital and technology to produce enough capital stocks in the first category and needs to import advanced equipment and technologies. In an extreme scenario, the domestic economy produces only consumer goods and non-tradable investment goods and imports all tradable investment goods from foreign countries.

Since the cost of capital (i.e. the interest rate) is lower than the current MPK, all the available funds that include firms' profits and workers' savings will be used in investment. In the early paradigm-changing growth stage, as shown by the Solow-Swan growth model (Swan 1956; Solow 1956), replenishing depreciated capital stocks takes only a small part of the output; therefore, the growth rate of the economy is roughly proportional to the growth rate of the capital and the corresponding growth of the labour force in employment. It is likely that the output-to-labour ratio Y/L has an S-shaped relationship with the ratio between capital and labour $k = (K/L)$ (Figure 2.3), and paradigm-changing growth can be divided into three phases: incubating, growing and mature phases. When k is small during the incubating phase, the MPK is small. As k increases to a level in the growing phase, MPK increases to a high level and there is almost a linear relationship between Y/L and k with a steep slope. When k increases to a level in the mature phase, MPK decreases to a low level again. The economy will enter the normal growth stage from the mature phase. China's economy before 1978 can be viewed as the incubating phase and since 1978 the growing phase. In the following mature phase, China's growth rate will drop to a level comparable to those of developed countries.

The domestic economy is in the growing phase, not only an increase in L with a constant K/L will maintain a constant high MPK, but also an increase in K/L will also maintain a relatively constant high MPK before the economy moves into the mature phase. The increase in L with a constant K/L will increase the income per capita in the domestic economy, because the working population in the reserve labour pool is still on subsistence farming in the rural

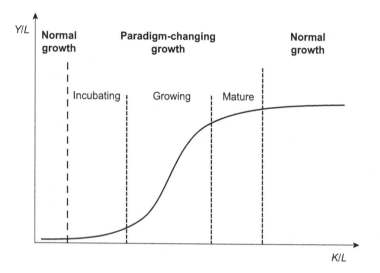

Figure 2.3 Relationship between the output-to-labour ratio *Y/L* and the capital-to-labour ratio *K/L*

Note: The slope of the curve at each point is the MPK which depends on the corresponding *K/L*. The paradigm-changing growth stage of economic development can be divided into three phases: incubating, growing and mature.

areas. The growth rate of the economy equals the sum of the growth rate in *K/L* and the growth rate of labour. When the population in the domestic economy is roughly constant, the growth rate of the economy is equal to the growth rate of the capital stock. Before the workers in the first age group in this growing phase start their retirement, the capital stocks bought with their savings would not be decumulated. Therefore, the growth rate of capital is larger than the current MPK, so that the GDP growth rate will be larger than the MPK. If the MPK = 10%, the GDP growth rate will be more than 10% per year.

The domestic labour market is in equilibrium when the domestic demand for labour is equal to the domestic supply of labour, $L_D = L_S$. In the growing phase, the demand for labour is mainly determined by the GDP because the wage rate required by workers in the rural reserve labour pool is so low that the labour demand curve becomes effectively a vertical line in the range of wage rates relevant to employers' hiring decision (Figure 2.4). An increase in the demand is like a parallel shift of the vertical demand line to the right. As the GDP grows further and the equilibrium wage rate increases with the GDP, the labour demand curve will gradually become noticeably downward sloping.

Since the domestic economy in the growing phase will mainly invest in capital stocks for producing consumer goods, the output that cannot be

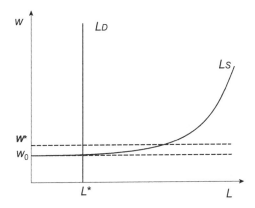

Figure 2.4 The labour market equilibrium

Note: L_S labour supply curve; L_D, the labour demand curve; w_0, the minimum wage rate required by the rural reserve labour pool; w^*, the efficient wage rate actually paid by employers. The number of workers demanded is almost solely determined by the GDP via the production function.

consumed by the workers (and firms for some domestic investment goods) has to be exported. When the real interest rate is zero (for most time since the reform, the real interest rate for deposits is negative) and time discounting factor is 1, if the workers starting work at 20 and retiring at 60 save for a possible longevity of 100 years, $s = (T - T_W)/T$ where T is the sum of working (T_W) and retirement periods in years, they will save 50% of their wage incomes.

Given the Cob-Douglas production function, $Y_t = K_t^\gamma L_t^{1-\gamma}$ when $\gamma = 1/3$, the workers will have 2/3 of the income. In such a case, saving 50% of their wages implies that 2/3 of the output (including the 1/3 that is the firms' profits) can be reinvested in the domestic economy. If Y_t consists of only consumer goods, the domestic economy needs to export 2/3 of its output and import investment goods worth 2/3 of its output for a balanced current account.

2.4.2 The foreign exchange market and economic growth

The scenario of exporting consumer goods and importing equal worth investment goods in the preceding section cannot maintain sustained high growth rate. As the exports of consumer goods will drive down their international market price and drive up the exchange rate of the domestic currency, the foreign demand for the domestic products will decrease. Importing large quantities of investment goods without an increase in the demand especially in foreign demand for the domestic goods will lead to a fast increase in K/L

ratio, moving the domestic economy into the mature phase in terms of the *K/L* ratio without achieving fast growth in the GDP per capita. The solution to this is to maintain the competitiveness of the domestic products by exchange rate control.

By setting the exchange rate of the domestic currency lower than its market equilibrium rate, the central bank increases money supply and imposes an additional national saving ΔS_t that is not invested in the domestic economy. The additional national saving equals the increase in the foreign exchange reserves held by the central bank. The proportion of this foreign exchange control induced national saving in the domestic GDP is $\dfrac{\Delta S_t}{Y_t} = \dfrac{\Delta M_t}{Y_t + \Delta M_t}$. The increased money supply (ΔM_t) will increase the price level, and decrease the real interest rate and the real exchange rate, and often the nominal interest rate and the nominal exchange rate will decrease as well. Figure 2.5

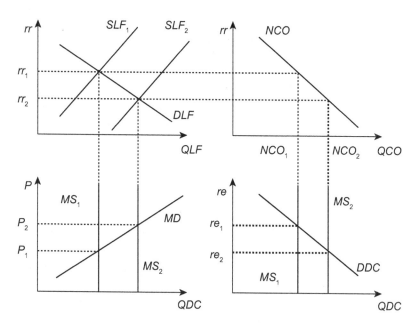

Figure 2.5 Effects of exchange rate control on the real exchange rate

Note: The real interest rate, the net capital outflow and the price level. An increase in domestic currency from MS1 to MS2 to buy foreign currencies will decrease the real exchange rate, increase net capital outflow and decrease real interest rate. DDC, demand for domestic currency; DLF, demand for loanable funds; MD, money demand in the domestic economy; MS, money supply in domestic currency; NCO, net capital outflow; P, price level; QCO, quantity of capital outflow; QDC, quantity of the domestic currency; QLF, quantity of loanable funds; re, real exchange rate; rr, real interest rate; SLF, supply of loanable funds.

illustrates the impact of increasing money supply to buy foreign currencies on the real exchange rate, the real interest rate, the net capital outflow and the price level. When the inflation rate does not increase proportionally with regard to the decrease in the real exchange rate and the real interest rate, the nominal exchange rate and the nominal interest rate will decrease.

The real-world situation has been very similar to this model, with the high growth in Chinese exports leading to large and persistent current account surpluses. The PBOC maintains control over fluctuations in RMB's exchange rates by purchasing foreign-currency revenues from exporters at prevailing exchange rates, with the purchases financed by either issuing domestic currency or bonds. Issuing domestic currency to purchase export-ers' foreign-currency revenues results in an expansion of money supply.

2.4.3 *The foreign economy and the domestic economic growth*

Exports to the foreign economy play an important role in this high saving rate and high investment rate economy. Exports occur only when foreign countries want to import. The demand from foreign countries is determined by three factors: 1) the price difference between the two economies; 2) dif-ferentiation between products of the two economies; 3) familiarity with the imported goods.

In the present model, the products from the domestic economy can only replace the traditional sectors of tradable goods, and these sectors grow proportional to the GDP growth of foreign countries. It will take time for exports from the domestic economy to take over the market of the importing countries, because the following constraints:

1 The output of the domestic economy: if foreign countries buy more goods from the domestic economy than it can export, the domestic price will increase so much that the goods are no longer competitive.
2 The familiarity of foreign importers and consumers with the goods from the domestic economy: when they are not familiar with the domestic products, they are less likely to import, even if the price is cheaper and the domestic economy can meet their demand if they have such demand.
3 Trade restrictions: foreign countries may impose trade restrictions to pro-tect their traditional industries.

It is most likely that the familiarity with domestic products is a function of the quantity imported with an S-shaped curve like that of Figure 2.3. When exports are small, the familiarity increases very slow, then increases very steeply, and finally increases in a much slower pace again. During the steeply increasing period, the exports of the domestic economy grow rapidly, due to its cheap price and production capacity as well as foreign countries' increasing familiarity with its products. Once the exported goods have occupied most of the market share of foreign countries' traditional tradable sectors, the exports of the domestic economy can only grow with the GDP of foreign countries.

2.5 Implications of the model

The present interest rate control model is a simplistic model for explaining the rapid economic growth of China since 1978, emphasizing the role of the high saving rate. It differs from general equilibrium models in that 1) the interest rates are decreed by the central bank rather than determined by the demand and supply of loanable funds; 2) the exchange rates are controlled by the central bank rather than by the market; 3) a large reserve labour pool exists and workers of agricultural residence register in this pool are neither unemployed nor employed; they usually accept lower wage rates than people with urban residence register because their farming income is much lower than the low wages of migrant factory workers; they could not choose to live in urban areas without having a job there. Figure 2.6 summarizes the interactions between the agents.

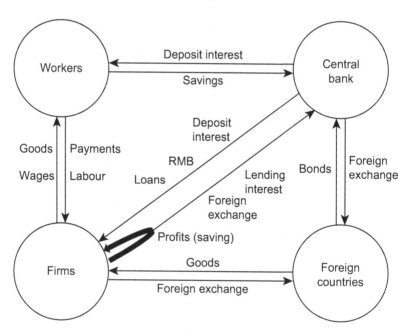

Figure 2.6 Interactions between agents in the interest rate control growth model

Note: The central bank represents the banking system, while firms represent both firms and their owners.

The interest rate control model is very effective in achieving high saving rates and consequently high GDP growth rates before the economy reaches its steady state described in the Solow-Swan model. However, it also implies that economic growth based on the increased saving rate will disappear when the steady state is reached and only technological progress can lead to continuous growth. Although the Harold-Domar model does not reject the possibility of continuous growth due to high saving rates, since the model assumes an unrealistic constant MPK, it seems unlikely that the interest rate control model can support continuous high growth rates.

2.5.1 *Labour costs*

In this model, since the production function is constant returns to scale, a 10% increase in capital stock requires a 10% increase in the labour force to maintain a 10% growth rate of the economy. As the economy grows, if the same technology is used, more and more workers will be needed to keep a steady growth rate, which requires parallel increase in capital and labour force. The large rural population could supply the labour force needed for rapid economic growth for a period of time. The current model implies that at some stage of the development the reserve pool of labour force will be unable to supply low-wage workers whose range of wage rates makes labour demand curve effectively a vertical line. Then the increased demand for labour will drive up the equilibrium wage rates, and increased wages will decrease the competitiveness of the domestic products.

A large labour force reserve in the rural areas provides the low-wage labour supply for China's fast growth since 1978. The first 30 years of China's reform is essentially a process of reducing social welfare and increasing the profitability of firms until the implementation of the *Labour Contract Law* on 1 January 2008. The lack of social welfare system and the low interest rate on domestic savings lead to a high marginal propensity to save for precautionary/buffer-stock savers. The deposit interest rate makes money too cheap for entrepreneurs not to invest in more stock of capital. As net exports grow, the surplus in the current account grows as well, which will lead to appreciation of domestic currency if exchange rates are market determined and reduce the surplus in the current account. The domestic currency, spent for buying foreign currency in order to hold down the exchange rate, will increase money supply in the domestic market, leading to more inflation.

2.5.2 *Foreign demand*

In this model, a substantial part of the increased output from domestic economic growth needs to be exported. However, when the export growth of the domestic economy is much faster than the economic growth in foreign countries, the overseas markets for the exported goods will be saturated at some point. The current model implies that, at that point, the exports of the domestic economy can only grow at the same rate as the foreign economies or slower, and the domestic economy cannot grow much faster than foreign countries if the domestic demand does not grow faster than foreign countries' economic growth. The combination of saturated foreign demand and increased labour costs as well as competition from countries with even lower production costs will make the export-led economic growth an ineffective approach for further economic development.

2.5.3 *Interest rate*

In this model, the central bank will not allow the workers to invest in foreign assets, and a lower domestic interest rate on deposits will decrease workers' interest income from their savings and probably increase their saving rates, leading to lower domestic consumption. A lower domestic interest rate on deposits stimulates investment because of lower capital costs. However, below-the-equilibrium interest rates cause inefficient allocation of capital and overinvestment leads to wasted production capacity eventually. A banking system guaranteed by the central bank via decreed deposit and lending rates to be profitable cannot be an efficient banking system in the long run. The current model implies that overinvestment will either drive down the MPK to the level of the domestic interest rate whereby the equilibrium interest rate is equal to the administered rate and the interest rate control is no longer needed, or cause economic crisis via overproduction or financial instability. The growth promoting role of below-the-equilibrium interest rates depends on 1) a large reserve pool of low-wage labour force and 2) a nascent exporting sector which has just started to explore the overseas market. When the large reserve labour pool disappears and the overseas market becomes saturated with products exported from this economy, setting interest rates artificially below the equilibrium rates cannot promote economic growth. The removal of the ceiling for deposit rates on 23 October, 2015 by the PBOC indicates that the difference between the MPK and the benchmark interest rates has become much smaller. The continuing publication of benchmark rates by the PBOC suggests that interest rates in China are still not fully determined by the market. When overcapacity pushes the MPK below the benchmark interest rate, most manufacturers will have difficulty to pay back their debts and banks' non-performing loans will increase.

2.5.4 *Exchange rate*

In this model, as the domestic output increases, net exports need to grow, which leads to a growing surplus in the current account. The central bank buys foreign currency at high rates in terms of domestic currency to prevent appreciation of domestic currency and maintain the competitiveness of domestic products, which leads to a large foreign exchange reserve by the central bank. The current model implies two possibilities: 1) exchange rate control will no longer be needed when overinvestment eventually equates the equilibrium interest rate with the administered rate; and 2) the process to keep home currency at low exchange rates artificially can no longer carry on because an artificially low exchange rate leads to inefficient allocation of resources. An artificially low exchange rate subsidizes overseas consumers at the expense of domestic consumers. Since the exchange rate will adjust sooner or later, the larger the foreign exchange reserves become, the higher the pressure for home currency to appreciate, the larger the financial loss when the exchange rate adjusts.

There might be another scenario in which the RMB depreciates. If overinvestment and inefficient allocation of resources lead to an imbalance so severe that causes an economic crisis to readjust at some time point, the capital outflow caused by panic might reduce the foreign exchange reserve sharply, leading to a large drop in RMB's exchange rate. Sometimes the expectation of an economic crisis might be sufficient to cause capital flight, which may then trigger a financial crisis followed by an economic crisis. Restrictions on capital flow can attenuate the effects of capital flight.

2.5.5   *Capital stock and capacity utilization rate*

Since the interest rate is much lower than the current MPK, underutilized production capacity can still make a profit, which leads to severe overinvestment especially when the domestic economy reaches the later stage of its growing phase. Overinvestment leads to low capacity utilization rate, which is a waste of resources. The increasing overcapacity will reduce the MPK gradually to the level of interest rate.

When most Chinese households were buying their first television, first washing machine, first refrigerator and their first car in the past four decades, the demand growth would be stronger than those in developed countries where households only replace these home appliances. After most households have owned those appliances, the demand for them will decrease because it has changed from mainly first-time buyers to mainly replacement buyers. Since manufacturers have increased their production capacity to meet the previous fast growing demand, the decrease in demand for those appliances will lead to severe overcapacity and cause the manufacturers operational difficulties in a very competitive market. China has been facing a severe overcapacity problem since 2013, especially in iron and steel, coal and non-ferrous metals, partly because the 4 trillion RMB stimulus package in 2009 following the global financial crisis further exacerbated the existing overcapacity.

The State Council was concerned with the sectoral overcapacity issue as early as in 2005. It issued on 2 December 2005 the *Interim Provisions for Promotion of Industrial Structural Adjustment* which was approved by the 112th Executive Meeting of the State Council on 9 November 2005, and called to restrict and eliminate production capacity based on out-of-date technologies and to develop new technologies. On 12 March 2006, the State Council issued the *Notice on Accelerating the Structural Adjustment of Industries with Excess Capacity*. The 2015 Economic Work Conference of the CPC Central Committee listed resolving excess capacity as the first of the five main tasks for 2016, and it has been one of the main economic tasks for the government since then. Reducing excess capacity has been a key component of the supply-side structural reform advocated by Xi Jinping, President of China and General Secretary of the CPC Central Committee.

2.6   Summary

In this chapter we have introduced a model of interest rate control as an explanation for China's rapid economic growth. This model looks into the contribution of low interest rates to economic growth through increasing domestic saving and investment. When the central bank sets the interest rate far below the current MPK or the equilibrium interest rate, the entrepreneurs will not only use their own income to invest in new capital stock, but also borrow as much as possible from the banks to use workers' savings for investment until the MPK equals the interest rate. High-level investment activities boost economic growth and introduce new technologies into the economy, which in turn promote growth in labour productivity. As the current MPK is much higher than the interest rate, the output growth is much faster than consumption growth, and exports become an important part of the economy. However, the allocation of resources might not be efficient when interest rates are not determined by market. The high-level investment by firms that have access to cheap bank loans will cause overinvestment and overcapacity. The overcapacity is solved by fast export growth and subsidized by the below-equilibrium interest rate. The reliance on exports to resolve overcapacity requires low exchange rates of the domestic currency RMB, which leads to China's huge foreign exchange reserves. Once the foreign market has been almost saturated by Chinese exports, export growth can no longer be faster than foreign economic growth and export will cease to be an engine for China's rapid growth. The increasing overinvestment will eventually lead to a level of overcapacity that drives the MPK equal to or even below the interest rate and eliminates the economic profits of the sectors. Many firms of the sectors with excess capacity will operate at a loss. As China's economy approaches its dynamic equilibrium, its investment will become less efficient in increasing output and its overall economic growth will slow down.

Appendix 2.A
The Solow-Swan growth model

The Solow-Swan growth model was developed independently by Robert Solow and Trevor Swan in 1956. This model extended the Harrod-Domar model by adding labour as a factor of production. In the Harrod-Domar model, capital-output ratios are not fixed, so the growth rate is determined by the saving rate and capital depreciation rate. The output of firms and the economy in any period t is determined by the production function

$$Y_t = F(K_t, L_t) \tag{A1}$$

K_t is the capital stock and L the labour force employed in the economy at period t. The production function $F(K_t, L_t)$ shows constant returns to scale in the two factors, that is, for any number ξ,

$$\xi F(K_t, L_t) = F(\xi K_t, \xi L_t)$$

The output of constant return production function equals the sum of factor marginal products multiplied by factor inputs:

$$Y = F(K, L) = F_K(K, L)K + F_L(K, L)L \tag{A2}$$

The marginal products of capital and labour, Y_K and Y_L, depend only on the capital–labour ratio, $k \equiv K/L$. Because $Y = F(K, L) = LF\left(\dfrac{K}{L}, 1\right)$

$$Y_K = F_K(K, L) = f'(k) \tag{A3}$$

$$Y_L = F_L(K, L) = f(k) - f'(k)k \tag{A4}$$

In the above equations, $f(k) \equiv F\left(\dfrac{K}{L}, 1\right) = y$ is the per worker production function which has a diminishing return in k, the capital stock per worker.

The increase in capital stock (net investment I) per worker; Δk, in period t is equal to the difference between the saving per worker and the depreciated capital stock per worker,

$$\Delta k = sf(k) - \delta k \tag{A5}$$

Equation (A5) defines the basic relationships between the outputs, saving and capital stock per worker in the model, where s is the saving rate and δ the depreciation rate. Figure 2.A1 illustrates how the steady-state equilibrium is achieved with $f(k)$, $sf(k)$ and δk. Saving in excess of depreciation will increase capital stock and in turn increase output. However, because depreciation increases linearly in capital stock, while output increases in capital stock with diminishing return, the depreciation will eventually reach a level

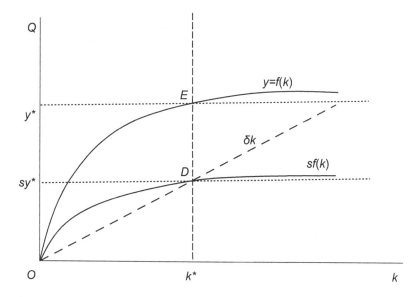

Figure 2.A1 The Solow-Swan model

Note: Q indicates the quantity of output per unit of labour, k the capital stock per unit of labour, δk the depreciated capital stock unit of labour, and $f(k)$ the output per unit of labour. At D, the saving reaches its steady-state level, $sy^* = sf(k^*) = \delta k^*$, and the capital stock reaches its steady-state level k^*. The corresponding steady-state output is y^* at E.

where the saving can only replenish the depreciated capital stock and the capital stock ceases to increase. This level is called steady-state equilibrium and the output per capital will no longer increase. Further growth requires technological progress to change production function $f(k)$. A too high saving rate will cause dynamic inefficiency, when a large proportion of output is used to maintain a large capital stock such that the consumption has to decrease from its optimal level.

The growth rate of the economy when the population in the domestic economy is roughly constant is

$$g_{GDP} = g_{K/L} + g_L = g_K \qquad (A6)$$

In equation (A6), g_{GDP} is the GDP growth rate, $g_{K/L}$ the growth rate in K/L, g_L the growth rate in L, and g_K the growth rate in K. Because the population is roughly constant, the growth rate of GDP per capita will be similar to g_{GDP}.

Appendix 2.B

The growth through interest rate control model

2.B1 The Agents

Workers, firms, the central bank and foreign countries are agents in this growth through interest rate control model. A representative worker's objective is

$$\max U = \sum_{t=1}^{T} \rho^{t-1} u(C_t) \tag{B1}$$

subject to

$$Q_t = (1 + r_t)(Q_{t-1} + W_{t-1} - C_{t-1})$$

$$W_t = PW_t \cdot V_t$$

$$PW_t = (1 + g_{PWt}) PW_t N_t$$

In equation (B1), U is a representative worker's lifetime utility, T the length of worker's working life plus retirement life measured in years, ρ the time discounting factor, $u(C_t)$ the one period utility, C_t the consumption in period t, Q_t the stock of physical net wealth, r_t the interest rate earned on the worker's savings, W_t the wages, PW_t the permanent labour income (Friedman 1957; Carroll 1997), V_t the white noise multiplicative transitory shock to income with mean value of one, g_{PWt} the growth rate of the permanent labour income and N_t a lognormally distributed white noise mean one multiplicative shock to permanent income. Workers deposit their savings in the bank for return of interests.

The objective of a firm is to maximize its net present value which is a function of its discounted future profits. The net present value (NPV) at period t,

$$NPV_t = \sum_{u=t}^{\infty} \frac{E_u}{(1+r)^{u-t}} \tag{B2}$$

In equation (B2), E_u is the firm's profit in period u. The firm has the production function described by equations (A1)–(A4) in the Solow-Swan model in Appendix 2.A. For simplicity, we assume that all profits of the firms are part of the national savings.

The objective of the central bank is to maximize the GDP. The foreign countries buy goods from the firms in the domestic economy by paying foreign currencies and sell bonds to (i.e. borrow money from) the central bank of the domestic economy by paying the international interest rate.

2.B2 The markets

There are six markets in the model. In the domestic commodity and service market, the aggregate demand is

$$D_D = GDP - NX = I + C = KY_K + LY_L - NX \tag{B3}$$

$$I = (1 - \varphi\theta r)KY_K + sLY_L - d\theta Y_K \tag{B4}$$

$$C = (1 - s)LY_L + \varphi\theta rKY_K + d\theta Y_K \tag{B5}$$

$$W = LY_L$$

In the above equations, D_D is the domestic demand, φ the proportion in workers' savings that belong to the retired workers, θ the proportion of the capital stocks that are bought with savings and d the decumulation rate of workers' saving invested in the capital stocks due to the retired workers consuming more than the returns earned on their savings. Before the workers in the first age group in this growing phase start their retirement, we have from equation (B4),

$$I = KY_K + sLY_L$$

As $sLY_L > 0$, the growth rate of capital is larger than the current marginal product of capital Y_K, so that the GDP growth rate will be larger than Y_K.

The aggregate supply to the domestic market is

$$SS_D = GDP - NX = Y(K,L) - NX = KY_K + LY_L - NX \tag{B6}$$

In the above equation, SS_D is the domestic supply. The price of a commodity at the domestic market is determined by its domestic demand and domestic supply.

In the international commodity and service market, the demand from foreign countries is

$$D_F = D_F\left(eP_F - P_D, GDP_F, Fam\right) = D_F\left(eP_F - P_D, \tau GDP_F, Fam\right) \quad \text{(B7)}$$

In the above equation, D_F is the demand from foreign countries, P_D the domestic price, P_F the international market price, e the nominal exchange rate, GDP_F the GDP of foreign countries, τ the proportion of traditional tradable goods and services in the GDP and *Fam* the familiarity of firms and consumers in the foreign countries with the goods produced in the domestic economy.

The supply by the domestic economy to the international commodity and service market, SS_F, depends on the price difference between the international market price and the domestic price, trade and economic policies in the domestic economy and the domestic demand and GDP.

$$SS_F = SS_F\left(eP_F - P_D, Policy, D_D, GDP_D\right) \quad \text{(B8)}$$

The exports of the domestic economy are substitutes of the tradable goods and services in the foreign economy.

In the domestic labour market, the demand for labour, L_D, is determined by the output of the domestic economy, the GDP, and the wage rate, w.

$$L_D = L_D\left(GDP_D, w\right) \quad \text{(B9)}$$

The labour supply is determined by the wage rate and the reserve labour pool in the rural areas.

$$L_S = L_S\left(w, RLP\right) \quad \text{(B10)}$$

In the above equation, L_S is the labour supply and RLP the size of the reserve labour pool. The domestic labour market is in equilibrium when the domestic demand for labour is equal to the domestic supply of labour, $L_D = L_S$.

In the domestic financial market, the equilibrium interest rate r^* is equal to the optimal marginal product of capital, the optimal marginal product of labour as well as the international interest rate (fr),

$$r^* = Y_K^* = Y_L^* = fr \quad \text{(B11)}$$

In the international financial market, the national savings in one period (year), S_t, include the part of returns from foreign assets B_t that is not consumed,

$$S_t \equiv Y_t - C_t + fr_t B_t \quad \text{(B12)}$$

The current account surplus is

$$CA_t = B_{t+1} - B_t = Y_t + fr_t B_t - C_t - I_t \tag{B13}$$

From equations (B12) and (B13), we have

$$CA_t = S_t - I_t \tag{B14}$$

National savings in excess of domestic capital formation flow into net foreign asset accumulation. Rearranging equation (B13), we obtain

$$\left(1 + fr_t\right) B_t = C_t + I_t - Y_t + B_{t+1} \tag{B15}$$

In the foreign exchange market, according to the theory of purchasing-power parity, the long-run equilibrium nominal exchange rate should be

$$e^* = P_D / P_F \tag{B16}$$

Because of interest rate arbitrage, there should be interest rate parity,

$$\left(1 + r_t\right) = \left(1 + fr_t\right) E_t \left[\frac{e_{t+1}}{e_t}\right] \tag{B17}$$

In equation (B17), E_t indicates expectation at period t. By setting the domestic interest rate low, the central bank reduces the equilibrium wages of workers and increases their saving rate as well as the national saving rate, which decreases the real interest rate and increases capital outflow.

To set the exchange rate of the domestic currency below its equilibrium rate for increasing the competitiveness of domestic products, the central bank increases money supply and imposes an additional national saving ΔSt that is not invested in the domestic economy. The additional national saving equals the increase in the foreign exchange reserves held by the central bank.

$$\Delta S_t = CA_t = S_t - I_t = NX_t$$

The proportion of this foreign exchange control induced national saving in the domestic GDP is

$$\frac{\Delta S_t}{Y_t} = \frac{\Delta M_t}{Y_t + \Delta M_t} \tag{B21}$$

Appendix 2.C

Savings of the first-generation workers at their retirement

If there are n workers who are in employment for T_W years with wage growth rate g_W and saving rate s^* and their ages are evenly distributed, the present value at period 1 of an individual worker's total wealth from savings of her lifetime wage incomes is

$$Q^1_{T_W} = \sum_{t=1}^{T_W} s^* W_1 \left(\frac{1+g_W}{1+r}\right)^{t-1} \tag{C1}$$

The superscript 1 in $Q^1_{T_W}$ indicates the present value at period 1.

The individual worker's wealth at the beginning of retirement is

$$Q_{T_W+1} = \sum_{t=1}^{T_W} s^* W_1 (1+r)^{T_W} \left(\frac{1+g_W}{1+r}\right)^{t-1} = s^* W_1 (1+r)^{T_W} \left(\frac{1-\left(\frac{1+g_W}{1+r}\right)^{T_W}}{1-\frac{1+g_W}{1+r}}\right)$$

$$= s^* W_1 (1+r)^{T_W+1} \left(\frac{1-\left(\frac{1+g_W}{1+r}\right)^{T_W}}{r-g_W}\right) \tag{C2}$$

The total wealth of the same age group (i.e. workers born in the same year) is

$$Q_{T_W+1} n / T_w = s^* W_1 (1+r)^{T_W+1} n / T_w \left(\frac{1-\left(\frac{1+g_W}{1+r}\right)^{T_W}}{r-g_W}\right) \tag{C3}$$

The total wealth of all workers when the first age group start their retirement is

$$
\begin{aligned}
TQ_{T_W+1} &= s*W_1(1+r)^{T_W+1}n\left[\frac{\left(\dfrac{1+g_W}{1+r}\right)^{TW}}{g_W-r} - \frac{1}{T_W(g_W-r)}\sum_{t=1}^{T_W}\left(\frac{1+g_W}{1+r}\right)^{t-1}\right] \\
&= s*W_1(1+r)^{T_W+1}n\left[\frac{\left(\dfrac{1+g_W}{1+r}\right)^{TW}}{g_W-r} + \frac{1+r}{T_W(g_W-r)}\frac{1-\left(\dfrac{1+g_W}{1+r}\right)^{TW}}{g_W-r}\right]
\end{aligned}
\qquad (C4)
$$

Notes

1 The marginal product of capital (MPK) is the additional output produced by adding one unit of capital while other production factors remain unchanged.
2 Gross national savings are calculated as gross national income (GNI) less total consumption, plus net transfers. The GNI is the GDP plus its *income* received from other countries and minus similar payments made to other countries.
3 A pure process innovation changes the way in which a product is made without changing the product itself. In practice, many process innovations also involve product changes.
4 A pure product innovation creates a new or improved product without any change in the production process except that more inputs may be required. In practice, a new product usually requires some innovation in the production process.
5 Net saving is gross saving net of depreciation of capital stock.
6 Comparative advantage is when a person or a country produces a good or service for a lower opportunity cost than other people or countries. If Alice can produce 3 units of good A or 4 units of good B in one hour, and Betty can produce 5 units of good A or 10 units of good B, Alice has comparative advantage in good A, while Betty has comparative advantage in good B.
7 Certainty equivalence in the case of consumption and saving decision describes the situation that despite the existence of uncertainty, a household can make its decision as if there is no uncertainty.
8 Tradable goods and services are those which can be traded internationally, such as textiles, cars and agricultural products. Non-tradable goods are those which cannot be traded internationally, such as public services, hotel accommodation, real estate, construction, local transportation, and services where the demander and producer must be in the same location.
9 The marginal product of labour (MPL) is the change in output that results from employing an additional unit of labour.

References

Bai, Chong-En, Chang-Tai Hsieh, and Yingyi Qian. 2006. "The return to capital in China." In *National Bureau of Economic Research working paper No. w12755*, edited by National Bureau of Economic Research. New York: National Bureau of Economic Research.

Bell, Stephen, and Hui Feng. 2013. *The rise of the People's Bank of China: the politics of institutional change.* Cambridge, MA: Harvard University Press.

Bolt, Jutta, Robert Inklaar, Herman de Jong, and Jan Luiten van Zanden. 2018. *Maddison Project database.* www.ggdc.net/maddison.

Borensztein, Eduardo, and Jonathan D. Ostry. 1996. "Accounting for China's growth performance." *The American Economic Review* 86 (2): 224–228.

Carroll, Christopher D. 1997. "Buffer-stock saving and the life cycle/permanent income hypothesis." *The Quarterly Journal of Economics* 112 (1): 1–55.

Carroll, Christopher D., Robert E. Hall, and Stephen P. Zeldes. 1992. "The buffer-stock theory of saving: some macroeconomic evidence." *Brookings Papers on Economic Activity* 1992 (2): 61–156.

Carroll, Christopher D., and Andrew A. Samwick. 1998. "How important is precautionary saving?" *Review of Economics and Statistics* 80 (3): 410–419.

Chamon, Marcos D., Kai Liu, and Eswar Prasad. 2013. "Income uncertainty and household savings in China." *Journal of Development Economics* 105: 164–177.

Chamon, Marcos D., and Eswar S. Prasad. 2010. "Why are saving rates of urban households in China rising?" *American Economic Journal: Macroeconomics* 2 (1): 93–130.

Chang, Chun, Zheng Liu, and Mark M. Spiegel. 2015. "Capital controls and optimal Chinese monetary policy." *Journal of Monetary Economics* 74: 1–15.

Deaton, Angus S. 1991. "Saving and liquidity constraints." *Econometrica* 59 (5): 1221–1248.

Domar, Evsey D. 1946. "Capital expansion, rate of growth, and employment." *Econometrica, Journal of the Econometric Society*: 137–147.

Friedman, Milton. 1957. *A theory of the consumption function.* Princeton: Princeton University Press.

Goodfriend, Marvin, and Eswar Prasad. 2006. *A framework for independent monetary policy in China.* Washington: International Monetary Fund.

Harrod, Roy F. 1939. "An essay in dynamic theory." *The Economic Journal* 49 (193): 14–33.

He, Dong, and Honglin Wang. 2012. "Dual-track interest rates and the conduct of monetary policy in China." *China Economic Review* 23 (4): 928–947.

He, Dong, Honglin Wang, and Xiangrong Yu. 2015. "Interest rate determination in China: past, present, and future." *International Journal of Central Banking* 11 (4): 255–277.

He, Xinhua, and Yongfu Cao. 2007. "Understanding high saving rate in China." *China & World Economy* 15 (1): 1–13.

Jiang, Xianglin. 2012. "The funds transfer pricing system of commercial banks in China." *Journal of Finance and Economics* 8: 59–61.

Kotlikoff, Laurence J., and Lawrence H. Summers. 1981. "The role of intergenerational transfers in aggregate capital accumulation." *Journal of Political Economy* 89 (4): 706–732.

Kuhn, Thomas S. 1962. *The structure of scientific revolutions*. Chicago and London: The University of Chicago Press.

Lardy, Nicholas. 2008. "Financial repression in China." In *Peterson Institute for International Economics working paper no. PB08–8*, edited by Peterson Institute for International Economics. Washington.

Ma, Guonan, and Wang Yi. 2010. "China's high saving rate: myth and reality." *Economie internationale* (2): 5–39.

Ma, Qing-Ping. 2017. "Contribution of interest rate control to China's economic development." *Journal of Chinese Economic and Business Studies* 15 (4): 325–352.

Modigliani, Franco. 1986. "Life cycle, individual thrift, and the wealth of nations." *Science* 234 (4777): 704–712.

National Bureau of Statistics of China. 2011. *China statistical yearbook 2010*. Beijing.

Porter, Nathan, and TengTeng Xu. 2013. "Money market rates and retail interest regulation in China: The disconnect between interbank and retail credit conditions." In *Bank of Canada working paper 2013–20*, edited by Bank of Canada. Ottawa.

Skinner, Jonathan. 1988. "Risky income, life cycle consumption, and precautionary savings." *Journal of Monetary Economics* 22 (2): 237–255.

Solow, Robert M. 1956. "A contribution to the theory of economic growth." *The Quarterly Journal of Economics* 70 (1): 65–94.

Song, Michael, and Dennis T. Yang. 2010. "Life cycle earnings and the household saving puzzle in a fast-growing economy." In *Chinese University of Hong Kong manuscript*, edited by Chinese University of Hong Kong. Hong Kong.

Swan, Trevor W. 1956. "Economic growth and capital accumulation." *Economic Record* 32 (2): 334–361.

Zeldes, Stephen P. 1989. "Optimal consumption with stochastic income: deviations from certainty equivalence." *The Quarterly Journal of Economics* 104 (2): 275–298.

Zhang, Xiaohui. 2012. *China monetary policy*. Beijing: China Financial Publishing Housing.

3 The social planner's problem and institutional roles in China's growth

China's high saving rate can explain a large part of China's rapid growth, but the saving rate is determined externally in the Solow-Swan model which does not provide a mechanism that guides the government to control the national saving rate. The Ramsey model provides such a mechanism (Ramsey 1928). The central problem in the Ramsey model is how a social planner (in a centrally planned economy) can arrange consumption and saving such that the expected total utility of the current and future generations is maximized. Cass and Koopmans developed the Ramsey model and showed that representative agents with the same constraints and objectives could achieve the same maximization outcome through the market (Cass 1965; Koopmans 1969; Blanchard and Fischer 1989). In the Ramsey-Cass-Koopmans model, the saving rate is internally determined and optimized by the market. For China's leadership after 1976, the social planner's objective in the Ramsey problem became maximization of sustained economic growth.

When the social planner is competent and powerful enough to enforce its plan as in the Ramsey model, the optimal saving rate for the maximum growth is to reinvest (almost) all the GDP and leave only the minimum for consumption that is necessary to maintain the survival and reproduction of the labour force. An economy planned for maximum GDP growth should grow faster than a market economy where the representative consumer maximizes her own and her offspring's utility as in the Ramsey-Cass-Koopmans model. In reality, however, a government has to consider whether its plan will affect its own survival, which is the political constraint for the planner. Since supervision of the labour force is not costless, the social planner has to consider whether incentives would be more effective than supervision for maintaining high labour productivity. Supervision costs may be included in the transaction costs, which are *costs* in making any economic *trade* in a *market*. Since the Solow-Swan model and the Ramsey-Cass-Koopmans model mainly consider the equilibrium conditions of an economy, they have not considered the impact of transaction costs on a country's economic growth, nor have they considered the efficiency of investment and capital utilization.

With available labour, capital and technology, the four key conditions for economic growth are social stability, functioning markets, entrepreneurship and low transaction costs. Social stability and functioning market maintained by effective institutions are fundamental conditions for reducing transaction costs and promoting economic growth. China's rapid growth requires not only the central bank's decrees to maintain low interest rates and high saving rates for four decades, but also the institutions which enable the central bank to do so and reduce transaction costs that hinder economic growth. After 1978, while setting rapid economic growth as its objective and using all its resources for this objective, the government led by the CPC has maintained social stability, kept transaction costs low, allowed markets to function, and encouraged entrepreneurship to emerge. This chapter will investigate how China's institutions contribute to China's rapid growth. Section 3.1 presents the planner's problem and a framework of institution-mediated economic growth; Section 3.2 looks into how implementation performance is influenced by institutions; Section 3.3 examines China's institutions and social stability; and Section 3.4 summarizes.

3.1 The social planner's objective and two types of growth

In microeconomics, decision makers base their choices on maximization of their expected utility. However, it is not clear on what a nation-state bases its economic decisions because there is no consensus on what the social utility function of a nation-state is or should be. On the one hand, the mainstream microeconomics alleges that individual utility is ordinal such that social utility cannot be obtained by summing up individual utilities; on the other hand, the solution of the Ramsey problem requires summing up cardinal utilities from different periods (and implicitly from different individuals). In the real world, the success of a government or a national leader is often assessed by the country's economic growth, although most people even economists agree that the GDP cannot truly measure the quality of life in a country. The original Ramsey problem is a problem for a central planner to maximize the expected total utility of the present and future members of the society by choosing the optimal consumption rate or saving rate (Ramsey 1928; Blanchard and Fischer 1989),

$$\max U_0 = \sum_{t=0}^{\infty} \beta^t u\left(c_t\right) \tag{3.1}$$

Subject to

$$y_t = f(k_t) \qquad (3.2)$$

$$k_{t+1} = y_t - c_t + (1-\delta)k_t = s_t y_t + (1-\delta)k_t \qquad (3.3)$$

In the above equations, U_0 is the expected total utility (per unit of labour at the beginning; β the time discounting factor; $u(c_t)$ the one period utility (also called felicity) which is a function of c_t, consumption (per unit of labour) in period t; y_t the output (per unit of labour) in period t; $f(k_t)$ the production function, which is a function of k_t, the capital stock (per unit of labour) in period t; δ the depreciation rate of the capital stock; and s_t the saving rate. David Cass and Tjalling Koopmans have shown that the optimal path for the Ramsey problem in a decentralized market economy is the same as what would be chosen by a central planner (Cass 1965; Koopmans 1969).

If the planner's objective is to maximize the expected sustainable GDP growth rather than the expected total utility of the current and future members of the society, the optimal saving path would be different from that of the Ramsey-Cass-Koopmans model. The planner's problem with the objective for maximum GDP growth can be expressed as,

$$\max U_0 = \sum_{t=0}^{\infty} \beta^t y_t \qquad (3.4)$$

Subject to

$$y_t = f(k_t)$$

$$k_{t+1} = y_t - c_t + (1-\delta)k_t = s_t y_t + (1-\delta)k_t$$

A trivial solution to the problem is to have $s_t = 1$; that is, the output is all invested to increase the capital stock. Obviously the trivial solution is not feasible in real life because the workers and the central planner need to consume to survive. The optimal path has the highest possible saving rate.

Since high saving rates will lead to faster economic growth before an economy reaches its steady state or normal growth, economies with saving rates higher than that generated by the Ramsey-Cass-Koopmans model are capable of growing faster than a market economy with the Ramsey optimal solution. China's rapid growth can be understood as the consequence of a social planner taking the expected sustainable maximum GDP growth as its objective. In the Ramsey-Cass-Koopmans model, the current generation tries to maximize their own utility as well as their offspring's, such that the social optimal saving rate will be lower than the saving rate for maximizing

GDP growth rate. The main constraints for maximizing GDP growth rate by reducing consumption to the subsistence level are politics and incentives. In terms of politics, when the social planner saves too much for investment and leaves too little to the current generation for consumption, the current generation may overthrow the social planner. In terms of incentives, leaving too little for current consumption would disincentivize the current members of the society and lead to low productivity.

A GDP growth-maximizing outcome that reduces current consumption is unlikely to be a Pareto optimization process in which each party increases its utility without reducing another party's. To understand the role of institutions in promoting economic growth, we propose a framework of institution-mediated economic growth that includes four components: technological path (T), objective (O), implementation performance (P) and social stability (S). Institutions play key roles in all the four components of this TOPS framework. The technological path has been explored by the (most) developed economies, so the social planner needs to set a social objective which is to be realized along the technological path. The long-term outcome of realizing the planner's objective depends on its implementation performance and the social stability.

The production function is determined by the current technology and the technological progress path is mapped primarily by the most developed economies. These economies will generally have lower growth rates except when they lead a breakthrough in the dominant production technologies, such as in the first or second industrial revolution. Since they are the first to complete the adoption of new technologies and closest to the steady state supported by the current technological level, they have to invest more in developing novel technologies to lift the ceiling of their dynamic equilibrium, but outcomes of research and development are usually uncertain. The backwardness of developing countries becomes an advantage in terms of choosing the right course for rapid economic growth (Abramovitz 1990; Gerschenkron 1962). Generally speaking, the further away is a developing economy from the production possibility frontier at the current technological level, the faster is its potential growth rate to catch up with the most developed economies. However, learning by doing and economies of scale may manifest as increasing return to scale during the early stage of the transition from one technological level to the higher technological level, so that the initial growth rate (in the incubating phase) is often slower than that in the growing phase.

An economy's technology level determines its maximum output level. During its paradigm changing stage, its growth rate is mainly a manifest of its transition speed from one dominant technological paradigm to a new dominant technological paradigm. The transition proceeds via investment in new capital stocks that incorporate new dominant production technologies and via training workers who can efficiently use the new technologies in production or service. The process from near-zero capital stock to the steady-state capital stock described by the Solow-Swan model is mainly paradigm-changing growth, which can have a high growth rate based on high saving rates (Solow 1956; Swan 1956). Industrialization of an agricultural economy is such a paradigm-changing process. China's reform and opening are the continuation of its industrialization initiated in the 1950s and disrupted repeatedly by political movements and rash economic campaigns launched by the CPC leadership, especially Mao Zedong. The efforts to industrialize the economy before 1949 had been hindered by wars and social instability. Since the technological path has been mapped out by the most developed countries, developing countries like China have the advantage to use the existing technologies in their paradigm-changing growth.

Once the paradigm change is completed, the economy enters the stage of normal growth which depends on small incremental innovations in products and business processes. Since small incremental innovations also occur during the paradigm-changing stage, paradigm-changing growth and normal growth coexist during the paradigm-changing stage. As the paradigm change approaches its completion, normal growth emerges as the main feature of the economy. Normal growth can be accelerated by massive investment, but its efficiency is much lower. Economic historians often wonder why the GDP per capita in the world hardly increased before the industrialization and has grown rapidly since then. The reason is that the rapid growth caused by industrialization is a paradigm-changing growth. The near zero economic growth before the Industrial Revolution was the normal growth with incremental innovations in existing technologies and production processes. Since incremental innovations in industrialized economies can be diffused and adopted much faster than in agricultural economies, the normal growth in industrialized economies also has a faster pace than that in agricultural economies.

Since the technological path is largely determined by the global efforts especially the most advanced economies, setting economic objective is the primary decision of a developing country. The objective is what a society wants to achieve in the long run. It determines economic policies and relevant regulations. In a centrally planned economy, the objective is set by the central planner (the government). In a market economy, the objective of the society should be the summation of individual objectives through invisible hands. However, in market economies under authoritarian governments, the objective of the government still affects the economic performance because firms and households always operate under the laws and regulations made by the government. Even in democracies, governments also have their economic objectives such as sustainable economic growth at fastest possible rates. Government economic policies and regulations in democracies are also influenced more by the elites than the ordinary people, and economists are more likely to promote policies that benefit capital and enterprises. In China, since the Third Plenum of the Eleventh Central Committee of the CPC in December 1978, rapid sustainable economic growth has become the objective of the CPC. The local GDP growth becomes a key measure of a local leader's performance and a predictor of the person's promotion opportunity. In order to get a high GDP growth, local governments and their officials try all they can to attract foreign and domestic investment into their jurisdiction (Zhou 2007; Li and Zhou 2005). Internal incentives within the government have contributed to China's rapid growth. Local and provincial governments in China competed to reduce *barriers* to investment in order to boost economic growth.

As shown by the social planner's problem, if the planner's objective is maximization of GDP growth within the current technological paradigm, a high saving rate is necessary. As shown by previous studies, China's government has maintained a high saving rate for a long period and China's saving rate actually increases over this period of rapid economic growth (Ma 2017; Huang and Wang 2010). When the right economic growth path is clear, an authoritarian regime might be more efficient than a democratic regime in promoting economic growth, because the authoritarian regime may impose high saving rates on its citizens. A democratic regime has to win support from the voters who might prefer their current consumption to their posterity's consumption, such that the saving rate in a democracy is likely to be lower than that of an authoritarian country with rapid GDP growth as its objective.

To ensure that high saving rates will lead to high growth rates, the society needs social stability. An economy cannot grow in a complete chaos or anarchy, so some forms of law and order need to exist for an economy to grow, no matter whether they are imposed by conventions in a community, an elected government, a dictatorship or a group of bandits. The longer a society stays stable the more likely its economy has a higher level of productivity, given the same technology and resources. Wars and social upheavals are often the major destroyers of capital stocks in an economy, but they may also bring in new institutions that facilitate economic growth and remove old institutions that hinder it. While economic difficulties often bring about political changes, rapid economic growth may also cause political instabilities. When the majority of ordinary people feel that the pro-business and pro-growth policies mainly benefit the elites and enterprises, they would become discontent with the government's pro-business policy and want to have a larger share of the increase in the national wealth. Popular discontent may lead to political upheavals and the overthrow of the government. Many authoritarian regimes could not sustain their pro-growth policy, because they have to abandon or modify their pro-business and pro-growth policy to placate the disenchanted masses.

3.2   Implementation performance and transaction costs

High saving rates are essential for high growth rates in both the Ramsey-Cass-Koopmans model and the Solow-Swan model. However, neither does Ramsey-Cass-Koopmans model concern itself with how savings are efficiently transformed into capital stock and how labour and capital stock efficiently produce output, nor does the Solow-Swan model. They implicitly assume full efficiency in these processes. For simplicity and mathematical convenience, economic theories usually use models with frictionless markets in which there are no transaction costs between two parties, nor are there institutions that could impose a transaction upon any party who does not want the terms of the transaction. In the real world, however, neither assumptions are valid. Firstly, transactions involve both monetary and time costs, the transaction costs. Secondly, there might be institutions that help impose a transaction upon one party of the transaction such that the transaction may decrease its utility. The first violation of the frictionless market assumption exists in all real-world transactions, while the second violation exists usually in places where the rule of law and property rights are not well established.

With available capital, labour and technology, there are three factors that may influence the implementation performance of the social planner's objective: the efforts of employees, the transaction costs between counterparties, and the outcomes of transactions. The efforts of employees directly affect the efficiency of transforming savings into capital stocks and the efficiency of utilizing capital and labour in production. Sufficient monitoring and giving employees adequate incentives to ensure sufficient efforts add extra costs to business, but shirking by employees, who think they are not adequately compensated or they can free ride, cost business more. The inefficiency caused by bureaucratic rigidity and conservatism in the central planning system is also a lack of efforts in employees due to inadequate incentives. The misalignment between the interests of employees, (state and collectively owned) enterprises and the state before the reform imposed a systemic or institutional cost on China's economy. The increased SOE autonomy and managerial power during the early stage of China's reform and opening enabled managers who felt underpaid to enrich themselves at the expense of their enterprises. The self-enrichment by SOE managers caused huge losses of their enterprises and helped the growth of TVEs and private enterprises. The principal and agent problem in SOE governance was later solved by privatizing medium and small SOEs and sharply increasing managerial income of the remaining large SOEs.

Transaction costs can be divided into three broad categories: 1) search and information costs, which are spent in finding the availability of the required good on the market, its (lowest) price and its quality, etc.; 2) bargaining costs, which are spent during the process of reaching an acceptable agreement with the other party to the transaction; and 3) policing and enforcement costs, which are required to make sure the other party sticks to the terms of the contract. New institutional economists consider transaction costs vitally important to the understanding of economic activities and reducing them able to boost economic growth. According to Douglass C. North, institutions are key in the determination of transaction costs. Therefore, institutions that facilitate low transaction costs boost economic growth (North 1992).

Institutions are stable, valued, recurring patterns of behaviour. They include both formal ones (such as family and government) and informal ones. New institutional economists emphasize (informal) institutions as the set of rules in a society that incentivize certain behaviours over others because they present less risk or induce lower cost, and establish *path-dependent* outcomes (Pierson 2000). Social stability and the legal system ensured by the government and social conventions provide the safe environment for transactions and the instruments for enforcement of contracts, which would cost the relevant parties much more if they were all provided by markets.

With regard to the planner's problem, implementation performance involves 1) how to raise the saving rate; 2) how to incentivize workers (and managers and entrepreneurs) such that equipment and technologies can be more efficiently applied; and 3) how to reduce transaction costs such that savings can be transformed into capital stock rapidly and production can be started faster. To incorporate the performance issue into the planner's problem, we can modify the equations as,

$$\max U_0 = \sum_{t=0}^{\infty} \beta^t y_t$$

Subject to

$$y_t = f(k_t, m_t) \tag{3.5}$$

$$k_{t+1} = \alpha_t (y_t - c_t) + (1 - \delta) k_t = \alpha_t s_t (y_t, T_t, P_t, S_t) y_t + (1 - \delta) k_t \tag{3.6}$$

In equations (3.5) and (3.6), m_t is the motivational or incentive factor measuring a firm's management capacity; α_t the transformation efficiency from savings to capital stock; T_t the technological level; P_t the planner's implementation performance; and S_t the planner's ability to maintain social stability. The incorporation of a motivational factor into the production function $f(k_t, m_t)$ implies that workers need to be motivated to exploit the full strength of their equipment and technology (Lazear 2000), while the transformation efficiency α_t indicates that same saving rates may not result in the same growth rate even if two economies are at the same stage of development. The difference between $(y_t - c_t)$ and $\alpha_t s_t y_t$ is the investment in "inventory" or unfinished capital stock projects. The saving rate s_t is a function of y_t, T_t, P_t and S_t, and the output growth enables the increase of the saving rate (Modigliani and Cao 2004).

China has been very successful in maintaining high saving rates through increasing the proportion of the gross national income (GNI)[1] received by senior managers, entrepreneurs, enterprises and the state as well as reducing the proportion received by ordinary workers. Its low interest rate policy and prohibition of unofficial financing activities are some of the causes for its high saving rates over four decades (Ma 2017). Reduction of social welfare by removing state welfare directly or by privatizing small and medium SOEs, industrialization of university education, debt-financed investment supported by huge money issuance and inflation, and reliance more on indirect tax for government incomes have all contributed to raising and maintaining China's high saving rate (Chamon and Prasad 2010). China's tax system is heavily relying on revenues from turnover taxes[2] such as value-added tax, business tax[3] and consumption tax[4] (Brys et al. 2013). Turnover taxes discourage consumption of ordinary people, because it increases the price level. Indirect taxes like turnover taxes are regressive and borne proportionally more by ordinary households in terms of their incomes. China's turnover taxes make up 60% of the total tax revenues, which is much higher than the proportion of indirect taxes in developed countries. In China, personal income tax makes up only 11.5% of total tax revenues in 2016, while corporate income tax is 22.1%. As turnover taxes can be transferred to the consumers and low-income households spend a much larger proportion of their incomes on consumer goods, low income households in China bear a heavier tax burden than those in developed countries.

The gradual deregulation, marketization and privatization of small and medium-sized SOEs in China since 1978 made it possible to provide adequate incentives (m_t) to motivate entrepreneurs, managers and workers, to reduce transaction costs and to improve the transformation efficiency α_t. The transformation efficiency also depends on the output level, technological level, implementation performance of the institutions and social stability,

$$\alpha_t = A\left(y_t, T_t, P_t, S_t\right) \tag{3.7}$$

In addition to deregulation, marketization and privatization, China's government has proactively intervened in economic activities to accelerate business deals by imposing transaction terms that benefit enterprises and investors at the expense of ordinary residents. The expected outcome of a transaction or a project is the most important determinant of whether the transaction or project will be carried out. The government usually imposes unfavourable transaction terms on the counterparties of business developers, which accelerates the completion of transactions, reduces transaction costs to business developers, increases their expected profits, and helps them start more business development projects. All these measures promote economic growth.

In the debate on the China Model, its supporters have argued for an active role of the government in promoting economic growth, typified as industrial policies. Justin Yifu Lin is a chief advocate of government industrial policies and one of the main ideas of the new structural economics he is promoting is that government should identify and support promising new industries (Lin 2012). One of the obvious examples where China's government uses its power to accelerate business deals is the demolition of existing buildings for new housing development projects since 2001. Without the involvement of local governments in pressurizing the residents to accept low demolition compensation (O'Brien and Deng 2015), China's real estate industry would not have achieved its phenomenal growth between 2004 and 2013. The houses whose owners rejected the low compensation offers were usually vacated and demolished by force under administrative orders from the government (Zhang 2004). The state subsidies to designated key industries and high-tech industries can be viewed as an approach whereby the government determines market outcomes in favour of the firms and entrepreneurs. State subsidies for high-tech industries promote the growth of new industrial sectors that would not survive at the market. Such policies mainly benefit domestic manufacturers and entrepreneurs, because the state subsidies are financed through general taxation which reduces consumer surplus.

China's strong government can usually push through development projects that face strong opposition from residents affected by the projects. Over the four decades of reform and opening, the government has generally become more and more pro-business especially in supporting housing developers, large SOEs and high-tech firms (Dean, Browne, and Oster 2010). Regulations and measures to facilitate business are implemented to reduce transaction costs of firms at the expense of savers and owners of demolished houses. Open oppositions and protests to government-supported business development projects appear only in recent years. The CPC party organization, the government and the mass organizations controlled by the CPC can all work together to persuade, coerce and force residents to back down from a confrontation with the local government for a government-supported development project. For civil servants working in government departments or employees of public utilities, if they do not sign the agreement for transferring their houses or apartments to housing developers, they would be told to stay at home before they sign the agreement (O'Brien and Deng 2015). Using housing development as an example, we can understand the logic behind China's rapid growth. Government-enforced demolition and low compensation relocation save developers' time and production costs and increase their profits, which gives developers more incentive to expand. China's government also made many regulations that discriminate against tenants in many civil rights especially the rights for children's education, which force people to become homeowners.

Pro-growth authoritarian governments can raise national saving rates and stimulate economic growth by increasing the share of the GDP received by capital and entrepreneurs, keeping interest rates below the MPK and suppressing the demand for higher income from ordinary workers. The interest rate control we discussed in Chapter 2 is another case that the government (central bank) imposes unfavourable outcomes on savers for the benefits of enterprises and investors. Both the former Soviet Union and China had achieved fast economic growth under central planning, if the negative impact of China's political movements and irrational economic campaigns have been taken into account (Borensztein and Ostry 1996; Davies et al. 1994; Nove 1961). The Soviet Union had been the fastest growing major economy in the world between 1920 and 1950. Although the Soviet economy started to stagnate in 1970s, it was still the fastest growth major economy between 1920 and 1989 before the Soviet Union began to disintegrate in 1990 with the declaration of independence by Lithuania on 11 March 1990 (Figure 3.1). During the reform and opening, China's government has taken a role between a central planner like the Soviet Union government and pro-business authoritarian governments in Asia and Latin America.

Many authoritarian governments such as military dictatorships in Latin America during the 1960s and 1970s and the Asian tigers during the 1960–1990s have achieved some kinds of growth miracle (Krugman 1994). South Korea and Taiwan, both of which had long-period authoritarian regimes, had the highest growth rates with their economies growing 30-fold between 1950 and 2016. Mainland China, Hong Kong, Singapore and Japan have grown more than 10-fold (Figure 3.2). Hong Kong's success shows that

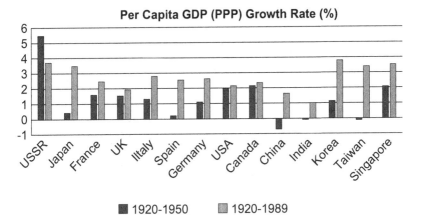

Figure 3.1 Per capita GDP (in 2011 constant international dollars) growth rates of some Asian, European and North American economies during 1920–1950 and 1920–1989

Note: Computed based on Maddison's database (Bolt et al. 2018). The Soviet Union (USSR) had the highest growth rate during 1920–1950 and the second highest during 1920–1989 among these economies.

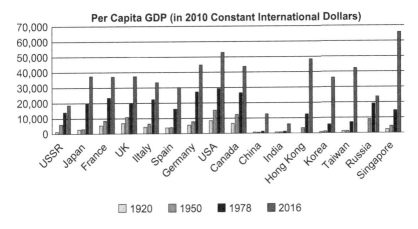

Figure 3.2 Per capita GDP (in 2011 constant international dollars) of some Asian, European and North American economies in 1920, 1950, 1978 and 2016

Note: According to Maddison's database (Bolt et al. 2018). There are no data for Hong Kong and Russia in 1920.

government only needs to provide law and order for markets to operate effectively and to implement pro-business policies; entrepreneurs and enterprises will find the optimal investment opportunities without guidance from the government. Before the transfer of sovereignty in 1997, Hong Kong British Authorities implemented a low tax pro-business policy. After Hong Kong returned, the government and the legislature are still not directly elected. In a certain sense, even though Japan is a democracy, its government might be considered authoritarian in managing its economy. The common feature of these growth miracles is their high investment rates through high saving rates or heavy borrowing. European and North American countries generally had a much higher GDP per capita than the Soviet Union in 1920, but the latter under the central planning system had caught up with many of them by 1950. However, the Soviet and Russian economy stagnated after 1978 when their per capita GDP approached US$15,000 to US$20,000, but the four Asian tigers continue to grow strongly after their per capita GDP exceeded US$20,000. It seems that centrally planned economy lacks efficiency during normal growth, while market economy, even under authoritarian regimes, could still be efficient during normal growth.

The lack of efficiency of the centrally planned economy during normal growth is partly due to its failure to take advantage of local talents, local initiatives, richness and salience of local information, and timeliness of local decision-making. Therefore, centrally planned economies tend to stagnate after a reasonably long period of rapid growth, even if the central planners have made their best efforts to stimulate growth. The higher implementation efficiency of centrally planned economies and authoritarian regimes during paradigm-changing growth is often not materialized for various reasons. Firstly, an autocrat may become overconfident and ignore basic economic laws. Secondly, a very low consumption rate is disincentive to employees even if it had not caused social unrests. Thirdly, rent-seeking, incompetency and corruption could be more difficult to rectify in an autocracy. In China, many regulations are made by officials to facilitate their own rent-seeking. State or collectively owned assets have often been sold below their market values by rent-seeking officials to entrepreneurs who have bribed them.

3.3   Social stability and institutional development in China

China's phenomenal growth depends on both institutions that ensure high saving rate and institutions that maintain social stability. Social unrests caused by discontent among some social classes toward inequality or corruption could bring down a pro-business government or force it to change its pro-business policy. Abandoning pro-business policy due to either regime change or policy change would scupper the rapid economic growth. The CPC leadership is fully aware of the importance of maintaining social stability to China's economic growth. On 26 February 1989, Deng Xiaoping told US President George W. Bush, "The overriding problem in China is the need for stability". Later he emphasized that "stability overrides everything", and maintaining stability has become a fundamental policy of the CPC leadership and the government since then. China's budget for maintaining stability is over CNY 760 billion in 2013, and it has been higher than China's defence budget in recent years (Wang and Lin 2014; Cao 2018). The budget for maintaining stability in 2019 is estimated to be nearly CNY 1.4 trillion (Qiao 2019).

Many people, especially those outside China, may wonder why Chinese people have tolerated government's pro-business practice especially in the case of violent demolition for new housing development projects. The popular obedience and tolerance can largely be understood from the history and culture of China. China had been a centralized autocratic country for over 2000 years since Qin Dynasty (221–206 BC) and Chinese people had to bear heavy economic exploitation and political suppression during this long history. The authority of the government and the cruel suppression of any oppositions maintained social stability before the accumulated discontents exploded into revolts and social upheaval. Confucianism, Taoism and Buddhism have also played important roles in stabilizing the Chinese society. The CPC has controlled almost every aspect of the society more efficiently than any dynasties and governments in China before 1949, which makes it more competent in fulfilling its objectives when it has adopted a right approach.

3.3.1 The leadership status of the CPC in China and political campaigns

The CPC's absolute control of the country ensures that setting rapid GDP growth as China's principal objective is feasible and social stability can be maintained in the long term. The leading role of the CPC in China's government came not from popular vote; the legitimacy of the CPC government like almost all earlier governments in China came from the victory over its opponents in civil wars or coup d'état. "The political power grows out of the barrel of a gun", as noted by Mao Zedong. After the establishment of the PRC, the CPC launched numerous political campaigns to transform the society and remould individual's ideology in order to consolidate the proletarian dictatorship, that is, the control of the country by the CPC. Between 1950 and 1978 there were over 50 nationwide political campaigns, many of which were intended to cleanse people considered not loyal to the CPC government, remould people into "new socialist persons" who will be loyal to the CPC, and make people religiously believe the greatness and correctness of the CPC leadership. Although these political campaigns per se have often severely hindered economic growth, they eliminated opposition to the CPC, enabled the CPC to control all aspects of the society, and paved the way for implementing pro-business policies and reducing social welfare and job security after 1978 without much resistance from ordinary people.

The Land Reform movement dispossessed and disgraced landowners and rich peasants who used to hold huge influence in China's rural society, and many landowners were killed. Poor peasants were encouraged to revenge on the landowners for alleged exploitation and oppression, and take over their assets and land. The drastic and often violent treatment of the landowners and rich peasants aligned the political stand and fate of poor peasants who were the rural majority with those of the CPC, and made poor peasants the social foundation of the CPC government in the rural areas. The Land Reform movement was launched during 1947–1949 in the CPC-controlled liberated areas and in 1950 nationwide. It was estimated that between one and two million landowners and rich peasants were beaten to death by activists or executed by the government in 1950. Some landowners might have behaved badly toward tenant peasants, but the majority of those killed were probably just because they were rich.

There were many cases in which rich supporters of the CPC or family members of the CPC cadres from rich families were cruelly treated or beaten to death during the Land Reform. Niu Youlan was one of them. Niu Youlan donated almost all his wealth to help the CPC-controlled troops during the War of Resistance against Japanese Aggression,[5] so he was considered an anti-Japanese patriotic gentleman by the CPC. Although he had little wealth left by the time of the Land Reform movement, activists pierced his nose with iron wire and let his son Niu Yinguan lead him with the wire like an ox (Niu is the Chinese character for ox) to parade through streets, because he was once the richest person in the Northwest region of the Shanxi Province. Niu Yinguan at that time was a middle ranking CPC cadre in charge of that region. Because of the humiliation, Niu Youlan refused to eat and died three days later. An underground CPC member and publicly anti-Japanese patriotic gentleman Liu Shaobai, who set up the Xing County Peasant Bank to help the CPC troops raise fund, was imprisoned for over 40 days and his younger brother Liu Xiangkun was beaten to death during the Land Reform. Liu Shaobai was released after intervention by Mao Zedong.

The Suppression of Counterrevolutionaries between late 1950 and 1953 physically eliminated many of those who were thought to be enemy by the CPC. Between 700,000 and 1 million people were sentenced as counter-revolutionaries and executed. Many of those executed were former officers of the Nationalist Party (Kuomintang, KMT)[6] government troops or former officials in the KMT government. Many of the former KMT officers switched side to the CPC or surrendered to the CPC troops when the CPC won the civil war. Some of the executed were actually underground CPC members working in the KMT government or troops, or even CPC guerrilla forces, but they were labelled counterrevolutionaries, KMT agents or bandits because of their complicated social relations. The famous writer Zhu Ziqing, once praised by Mao Zedong as a patriotic democratic fighter, had a son called Zhu Maixian who secretly joined the CPC in 1936. Later Zhu Maixian was instructed by the CPC to work in the KMT forces. He successfully persuaded the KMT forces in north Guangxi region to switch to the CPC side in late 1949. He was arrested, accused of being a bandit spy and executed in 1951. His superior, a KMT major general, Jiang Xiong, who led the side-switching to the CPC, was also executed.

The Intellectual Ideological Transformation movement during 1951–1952 remoulded Chinese intellectuals who historically played the role of social critics and the conscience of the society, and made them to comply willingly with the CPC ideology. In the movement, intellectuals were required to self-criticize their past wrong-doings, their despising of manual labour and their ideology of the exploiting classes. Some famous scholars had to redo their self-criticism several times because the masses (and the CPC organization) thought their self-analysis was not deep enough. The renowned mathematician Hua Luogeng could not bear the repeated requests for deeper self-criticism such that he attempted suicide. Intellectuals who used to be praised for defying and criticizing the KMT regime became more compliant in the new society.

In the Anti-Corruption, Anti-Waste and Anti-Bureaucracy ("Three Antis") movement from December 1951 to October 1952, many government officials were wrongly accused of various corruptions and forced to confess much-exaggerated or non-existent crimes. In the Anti-Bribery, Anti-Tax Evasion, Anti-Stealing State Property, Anti-Jerry Building and Anti-Stealing State Economic Intelligence ("Five Antis") movement from February 1952 to October 1952, many businesspeople were accused of those wrong-doings. There were 133,760 unnatural deaths during the two movements according to official data. The Five Antis humiliated and disgraced the bourgeois or capitalists as a respectable class in cities, and made them no longer have the enthusiasm to run their business and even less likely to disagree with the government. When the Government Administration Council (the name of the State Council between 21 October 1949 and 27 September 1954) issued the *Interim Regulations on Joint State-Private Industrial Enterprises* on 2 September 1954, many private business owners actively asked to become joint state–private enterprises.

The movement to Root-Out Hu Feng Counterrevolutionary Group in 1955 began to root out different views and opinions within the Marxist camp. Hu Feng was a Marxist literary theorist, poet and literary translator. He joined the youth branch of the CPC in the early 1920s and became a member of the Japanese Communist Party when he studied in Japan in the late 1920s. He had helped and coached some younger writers and poets, so that he had a following in the literary circle. Although he praised the communist cause enthusiastically in his literary works, he was often criticized by the CPC Central Committee Propaganda Department since the 1940s because his theory differed from Mao Zedong's view in some aspects. During the movement against Hu Feng, over 2000 people in literary and media circles, including many CPC members were affected, 92 arrested and 78 formally labelled as "Hu Feng group members". Hu Feng was arrested in 1955 and imprisoned for his opinions expressed in his report to the Politburo of the CPC Central Committee and in his private letters to his friends. He was sentenced to 14 years imprisonment retrospectively in 1965 and sentenced to life imprisonment in 1970 for writing "reactionary" poems. He was released from prison in January 1979. After the movement, intellectuals dare not to differ from the line of the CPC leadership.

In 1957, the CPC launched the Rectification Movement against bureaucracy, sectarianism and subjectivism, and asked people to expose shortcomings in the CPC's performance to help the CPC improve. When many people within and outside the CPC were mobilized and persuaded by the CPC to raise issues, criticize mistakes of the CPC officials and suggest policy changes, Mao Zedong started the Anti-Rightists Movement and labelled over 550,000 people "rightist", most of whom were intellectuals. Some people were labelled rightist because there was a quota and organizations had to fulfil their quota of rightists. Most rightists were stripped of their jobs, sent to labour campus or countryside to be reformed under supervision, and some died of starvation during the economic crisis in the early 1960s. The rightists received further persecutions during the Cultural Revolution. The Anti-Rightists movement made people more reluctant to express their opinions except praising Chairman Mao, the CPC, the people and the motherland.

Traditionally China's central government had limited influence in the rural areas and its administrative power reached only the county level. Rural villages were managed through autonomy of patriarchal clans or autonomy of squires. Mao Zedong's revolutionary strategy of using the rural areas to encircle the cities also reflects the weak influence of the KMT government in the rural areas. The Rural Socialist Education Movement, often called Four Cleans Movement, during 1963–1966 strengthened the control of rural areas by the CPC Central Committee. It began with "clean work points, clean accounts, clean warehouses and clean properties" in rural areas and then became "clean thinking, clean politics, clean organization and clean economy" in both urban and rural areas. The movement initially targeted the grassroots cadres who were considered corrupted and degenerate, and later former landowners, rich peasants, counterrevolutionaries, bad guys and rightists. The movement was guided by Mao Zedong's theory of class struggle as the key link. Many grassroots cadres and ordinary people were mistreated and beaten because of wrongly accused misconducts or exaggerated mistakes. Following the movement, cadres in rural areas had to toe the line of the CPC central committee cautiously, and ordinary people followed the line of the CPC central committee more faithfully.

The Cultural Revolution during 1966–1976 was launched by Mao Zedong as a decision of the CPC Central Committee. Initially many intellectuals in universities and schools as well as the former landowners, rich peasants, counterrevolutionaries, bad guys and rightists were targeted by "red guards" mobilized by the call from the CPC Central Committee and Mao Zedong. In August and September 1966, 1772 people in Beijing alone were beaten to death by the red guards. Several secondary school headmasters were beaten to death by their own students. Later the targets became CPC and government cadres who were thought to be capitalist roader in power. The president of China, Liu Shaoqi, second in the CPC hierarchy since 1945, was removed from all his CPC and state positions at the Twelfth Plenum of the Eighth CPC Central Committee held during 13–31 October 1968. He was imprisoned and denounced as the biggest capitalist roader who attempted to usurp the power of the CPC and the state, because he was considered not loyal to Mao Zedong.

Most CPC cadres at various levels were also denounced as capitalist roaders and agents of Liu Shaoqi's counterrevolutionary revisionist line. They were stripped of their power by revolutionary rebel forces and sent to do manual jobs in the "7 May" Cadre Schools, which were farms named after the 7 May Instruction. The personality cult of Mao Zedong swept China crazily, and people thought to be irreverent to Mao Zedong would be imprisoned and often executed. During the Cultural Revolution, over 4.2 million people had been locked up for investigation of their alleged mistakes, more than 1,728,000 died of unnatural causes, 135,000 people were executed as counterrevolutionaries, and over 100 million people were ill-treated. The Cultural Revolution made ordinary people more fearful of failing to follow the line of the CPC Central Committee.

3.3.2 *The communist ideology and organization as society stabilizing factors*

The communist ideology and the ubiquitous existence of the CPC organization are also essential to maintain social stability under the leadership of the CPC. Most of the early CPC members were idealists who wanted to create a society in which everybody, especially poor Chinese people, could live a happy life. Mao Zedong, who was ruthless in CPC inner-party power struggles and in CPC's power struggles with other political forces, was fascinated with ancient Chinese utopian thoughts and practices. He attempted to make China a rich egalitarian society in the way whereby he led the CPC force to the victory in the civil war. He emphasized that serving the people was the main objective of the CPC. Even though the political movements launched by the CPC had hurt many Chinese people, the early CPC members did believe in communism and tried to serve the people. Their idealism may explain the enthusiasm for economic construction in the CPC after the death of Mao Zedong. It may also explain why there was little corruption in the grassroots and middle-ranking CPC cadres from the establishment of the CPC government in 1949 to the early reform years up to the mid-1980s. With retirement of the idealistic early CPC members, rent-seeking and corruption among the new CPC cadres who grew up after 1949 became more and more rampant.

The CPC organization follows the Leninist principle, which requires the entire party to obey the party leadership. After an early period during which the Communist International and the Communist Party of the Soviet Union played a dominant influence between 1921 and 1938, the CPC established a political system centred on the personal authority of Mao Zedong after the Rectification Movement in Yan'an during 1942–1945. The CPC views armed struggle, party and its peripheral organization building, and propaganda with vital importance. Every village in rural areas, every company in the armed force and every factory with three or more CPC members would have a party branch with a secretary, an organization officer and a propaganda officer. In the CPC-controlled regions before 1949 and in mainland China after 1949, the CPC Party Secretary is superior to the administrative head of the government or non-governmental organizations at the same level. From the national level to the township level, governments are only the executor of decisions made by the CPC Central Committee and local committees.

Besides the CPC organization at each level, it has also set up mass organizations for various groups of people, such as youth, women, workers, peasants, and literary and art circles. Those organizations are closely guided and led by the CPC-leading group working within them. Moreover, the central planning system made everybody dependent on the government-controlled resources. The Unified Purchase and Unified Distribution enforced since 1953 means that one had to rely on the government ration of food for survival. A person could only work in the place where her or his residence registration was and the residence registration entitled her or him to one person's ration of food and other supplies for living. Except a few who still owned apartments or houses after the Land Reform and the Socialist Remoulding of Agriculture, Handcraft, and Industry and Commerce, the accommodation of urban residents was also provided by the state-owned institutions. The CPC controlled almost every aspects of life in China until the early 1980s.

Before 1978, a person who had aspiration for career progression in China had to become a CPC member. Even after the reform and opening, the CPC membership is still important for career progression in public sectors and it also brings economic benefits to private entrepreneurs (Li et al. 2007). All cadres in government offices and companies and officers in the armed force were appointed from the CPC members, except some ceremonial positions held by members of the so-called democratic parties[7] which existed before 1949 and aligned with the CPC as opposition parties to the KMT government (Brødsgaard 2012). These organizational arrangements ensure that the objective set by the government can be carried out speedily. Within the CPC, it is imperative that all members align themselves with the Central Committee ideologically, politically and operationally. The late state president Liu Shaoqi once called on all the CPC members to become tamed tools of the CPC. To individual CPC members with some independent thinking, the party organization will carry out ideological work to help them remould themselves ideologically. It usually involves severely criticizing an individual by a group of colleagues and persuading her or him to remorse by her or his friends under instruction of the party organization. Those unrepentant ones would be purged as anti-party elements and disgraced.

Besides the organizational requirement of CPC membership for government officials, military officers and factory managers, the CPC also tried its best to remould people's ideology according to what the CPC leadership wants people to be. People were indoctrinated to believe that they lived a much happier life than those in the capitalist countries and they should be grateful to Mao Zedong and the CPC who brought them the happiness. The political movements had also cleansed people of integrity who had the foresight to see the mistakes of the CPC and the courage to speak out. By the time of Mao's death, ordinary Chinese people were scared of unwittingly saying or doing something wrong which could bring misery and hardship to their families. Children from families of landowners, rich peasants, capitalists, counterrevolutionaries, rightists and persons with serious mistakes were discriminated in education, employment and promotion opportunities.

In order to indoctrinate people with the CPC ideology, the CPC felt it necessary to prevent people from knowing what capitalist countries were like. Foreign publications except for research and government information purpose were not allowed to enter China, and foreign radio broadcasting were jammed to make it difficult for Chinese people to receive. Secretly listening to radio broadcasting from unfriendly capitalist countries could be prosecuted as criminal offence. The control was gradually loosened since 1977 amid criticisms from Deng Xiaoping and some of the CPC old-timers on bourgeois liberalization. With the Internet becoming the main tool for acquiring information, China's government has implemented very strict control over the Internet to prevent people from obtaining information which the CPC leadership does not like. Popular websites such as Google, YouTube, Facebook, Twitter and many more media sites are blocked in mainland China and only accessible with virtual private networks (VPN). Domestic websites are shut down completely if they intend to spread views and information which the government does not want the general public to know. The government has also established sensitive word-filtering systems, which find and remove messages containing the sensitive words.

The communist ideology has played a key role in convincing ordinary people that current hardship is justified by the future happiness of their posterity. The ubiquitous existence of the CPC organizations and the unity of the CPC organization under its Central Committee enable the CPC leadership to promote economic growth more efficiently, when the leadership follows the basic economic laws and common sense. The capacity of the CPC to mobilize national resources could also lead to economic disasters when its leadership challenges the basic economic laws, for example, during the Great Leap Forward which caused widespread famine in 1960–1962 and a severe economic crisis with China's GDP shrinking by 31.3%.

3.3.3   *Chinese culture in ensuring social stability and high saving rate*

The Chinese culture has also helped the CPC and other ruling classes in history maintain social stability and manage this large country. The dominant thoughts in the Chinese history are Confucianism, Taoism and Legalism. The one most promoted by the ruling class is Confucianism, which advocates respect and obedience to the monarch, the parents and the superiors, as well as love and forbearance toward other people (Waley 2012). Taoism, which advocates harmony with nature and reality, laissez-faire in governance and personal inaction, is more influential with literati and officials, especially those who were frustrated or disappointed in their career. Legalism advocates strict laws and severe punishments against ordinary people such that monarchs would have unchallenged authority over their subjects (Waley 2005). Chinese rulers in history were usually Confucian in appearance and Legalist internally.

The original ideas of Confucianism on the relationships between parents and children or between monarchs and their subjects were bidirectional: parents are affectionate and their children obedient; monarchs are beneficent and their subjects loyal. Confucius (551–479 BC) argued that monarchs should rule by good virtue; that is, they should become a role model in decency and good behaviours for ordinary people. In the Confucian view, if monarchs behave well in virtuous ways, ordinary people will follow their suit and crimes will largely disappear. Mencius developed the idea that people are the most important, the statehood secondary to people and monarchs the least important of the three. According to Mencius (371–289 BC), if a monarch is tyrannical, people have the right to overthrow him. In historical reality, the ruling classes promoted more heavily the side of Confucianism that called for obedience to monarchs, superiors and parents (Shun 1997). Confucian teaching had been an important stabilizer of Chinese society, which seemed more stable than other societies under the same social and economic conditions. Without Confucian teaching as the official ideology, the history of China would have had more disruptions. Confucianism helped the dynasties in history enforce their will over ordinary Chinese people and made governance relatively smooth.

Confucianism preaches conscientious and rigorous working ethics. Zeng Shen (505–435 BC), a disciple of Confucius, said: "I examine myself each day on whether I have not worked whole-heartedly for my principal, whether I have not been trustworthy to friends, and whether I have not mastered the knowledge which I will teach my students". Although Confucianism regards learning the highest and praises people who are still optimistic under destitute conditions, it does not oppose commerce and merchants. Zigong (520–456 BC), one of the famous disciples of Confucius, was a very successful and rich merchant, and he played a key role in spreading Confucianism (Waley 2012). Confucianism thinks that it is normal for decent people to desire wealth, but wealth should be gained via proper means. Herman Kahn thinks that the Confucian ethic was playing a "similar but more spectacular role in the modernization of East Asia than the Protestant ethic played in Europe" (Kahn 1979).

Legalists advocate strong government and tough laws against ordinary people. According to Shang Yang (395–338 BC) who reformed the government system of Qin state during the Warring State period (475–221 BC), monarchs should control more wealth and make their subjects poor and ignorant, and use more punishments and give fewer rewards. When people are poor, they are more likely to follow orders from the government. When people receive more punishments, they are more grateful to a few rewards and more respectful to the government and monarch. Monarchs should use crafty persons to manage ordinary people so that they will be fearful to the government. If good persons are appointed to manage ordinary people, they will no longer respect the government (Duyvendak 1928). Legalists did not like merchants; they considered merchants as moths of the society, while fighters and farmers are useful people to the state. The merchant class had been discriminated in Qin state since the Warring States period, which was continued after China's unification by Qin Dynasty (221–207 BC) and the subsequent dynasties until middle Ming Dynasty (1368–1644 AD).

China's high saving rate is caused by China's culture of hard work and thrift as well as its economic policies (Garon 2011). The culture of hard work and thrift arose partly from the natural environment which requires hard farming for food and partly from the economic and political traditions. One poem during the Tang Dynasty (618–907 AD) says "there is no idle farmland in the world, but farmers still die of starvation". The hardship for ordinary people to make a living and Confucian teaching of moderation in spending cultivated the tradition of hard work and thrift. This is also true in other East Asian countries such as Korea and Japan.

The Confucian ideal society was Great Harmony or Great Unity in the world, in which everybody tries to do his or her best for the benefits of the community and the community cares for everybody (Confucius, Dai, and Legge 2013). Confucian scholars concede that it is difficult to reach Great Harmony with the political wisdom and competency of most real-world rulers. Generally people can only hope for a moderately prosperous society in which people work for their own benefits and social conventions made by sages effectively govern people's behaviour for stability and peace. The term "moderately prosperous society" was used by Deng Xiaoping in the late 1970s for describing the objective of China's reform and economic growth plan by the end of 20th century. The CPC Central Committee report at the Sixteenth CPC National Congress in 2002 put forward the goal of building a moderately prosperous society in all aspects. The CPC Central Committee report at the Eighteenth CPC National Congress in 2012 set the goal of completing the process of building a moderately prosperous society in all aspects by 2020.

The East Asian people historically have accepted Confucianism together with ancient Chinese culture, and they tend to have a pragmatic approach toward religions. They worship all gods that can bring happiness and good fortune to them, and lack the religious fervour manifested by Europeans or Semito-Hamitic people in history. In countries, especially developing countries, with several major ethnic groups, policies often divide according to ethnic lines and conflicts arise from opposing ethnic groups, religions or cultures. China has 56 ethnic groups, Han Chinese made up more than 97% of the total population until 1982, with the proportion dropping 91% because the one-child policy applied only to Han Chinese. The homogeneity of the population and the culture increases the cohesion of the country, which is a big advantage over countries with several major ethnic groups. East Asian countries China, Korea and Japan (which has Ainu people as an ethic minority) are all almost homogeneous in their people, language and culture.

3.4 Summary

In microeconomics, economic decision-making is based on maximization of expected utility, but utility levels between two individuals cannot be compared or added because utility in modern economics is primarily considered ordinal. In macroeconomics, there is no agreed social utility function for computing and comparing total social utility. The success of a country or its government has usually been measured by the GDP per capita or its growth rate. If the social planner's objective in the Ramsey problem is changed to maximum sustainable economic growth, the solution will not be reached by agents who want to maximize their offspring's as well as their own utility through market.

China's rapid growth can be understood as the problem of a social planner who want to maximize a country's sustainable growth rate, subject to its social stability, the motivation of agents to work toward the objective, and the implementation efficiency. High saving rates, efficient implementation of growth plans and social stability are the three key factors for China to catch up with more developed economies. Since 1978, China's government has implemented more and more pro-business policies and pushed through business development projects often at the expense of local residents. The performance of local government leaders has been assessed mainly on the economic growth numbers, which makes providing better business opportunities to attract investment the top priority of local governments.

The authority of the CPC, obtained from its victory in the civil war with the Nationalist government and many political campaigns, has enabled it and the government to maintain social stability, reduce monetary costs and bargaining time for enterprises in implementing business development plans, and sustain a high level of national saving and investment over a long period. The Confucian culture has also helped stabilize the society and encouraged self-reliance and entrepreneurship. These institutional factors complement the factors emphasized by the neoclassical economics, underlying China's rapid growth as well as the China Model.

Notes

1 The gross national income (GNI), also called the gross national product (GNP), is the the total value of goods and services produced within a country (the GDP) plus its income received from other countries (notably interest and dividends) and minus similar payments made to other countries.
2 A turnover tax is charged at a certain stage of production and sale of goods. In China, turnover taxes include value-added tax (VAT), business tax, consumption tax, and urban construction tax.
3 Business tax in China is charged on the revenue of firms which provide services, transfer intangible assets and sell real estate properties. It has been gradually

replaced by VAT since 2011 and abolished on 30 October 2017 by the State Council.

4 Consumption tax or excise duty in China is charged on the turnover of certain goods and services, especially luxury goods.

5 The War of Resistance against Japanese Aggression began on 7 July 1937 when the Japanese army launched an attack on Chinese troop in the suburb of Beijing and ended on 2 September 1945 when Japan formally surrendered to the Allied Forces. In recent years, the war is considered to begin on 18 September 1931 when the Japanese army launched an attack on Chinese troop in Shenyang and later occupied Manchurian region.

6 The Nationalist Party (Kuomintang, KMT) was originated from revolutionary groups against Qing Dynasty. It formed the National Government in Guangzhou on 1 July 1925, launched the Northern Expedition on 9 July 1926 which defeated Northern warlords who controlled the internationally recognized National Government in Beijing, and nominally unified the country on 29 December 1928. The National Government controlled by the KMT fled to Taiwan on 9 December 1949 after its defeat by the CPC in the civil war.

7 There are eight democratic parties in China: China Revolutionary Committee of the Kuomintang, China Democratic League, China Democratic National Construction Association, China Association for the Promotion of Democracy, Chinese Peasants' and Workers' Democratic Party, China Zhi Gong Dang, Jiusan Society and Taiwan Democratic Self-Government League.

References

Abramovitz, Moses. 1990. "The catch-up factor in postwar economic growth." *Economic Inquiry* 28 (1): 1.

Blanchard, Olivier J., and Stanley Fischer. 1989. *Lectures on macroeconomics*. Cambridge, MA: MIT Press.

Bolt, Jutta, Robert Inklaar, Herman de Jong, and Jan Luiten van Zanden. 2018. *Maddison Project database*. www.ggdc.net/maddison.

Borensztein, Eduardo, and Jonathan D. Ostry. 1996. "Accounting for China's growth performance." *The American Economic Review* 86 (2): 224–228.

Brødsgaard, Kjeld Erik. 2012. "Cadre and personnel management in the CPC." *China: An International Journal* 10 (2): 69–83.

Brys, Bert, Stephen Matthews, Richard Herd, and Xiao Wang. 2013. *Tax policy and tax reform in the People's Republic of China, OECD taxation working papers, no. 18*. Paris: OECD Publishing.

Cao, Cang. 2018. "How much is China's stabilization fund?" *Culture Crossings* (2): 16.

Cass, David. 1965. "Optimum growth in an aggregative model of capital accumulation." *The Review of Economic Studies* 32 (3): 233–240.

Chamon, Marcos D., and Eswar S. Prasad. 2010. "Why are saving rates of urban households in China rising?" *American Economic Journal: Macroeconomics* 2 (1): 93–130.

Confucius, Sheng Dai, and James Legge. 2013. *The book of rites*. Beijing and Washington: Intercultural Press.

Davies, Robert William, Mark Harrison, and Stephen G. Wheatcroft. 1994. *The economic transformation of the Soviet Union, 1913–1945*. Cambridge: Cambridge University Press.

Dean, Jason, Andrew Browne, and Shai Oster. 2010. "China's 'state capitalism' sparks a global backlash." *Wall Street Journal*, 16 November 2010.

Duyvendak, Jan Julius Lodewijk. 1928. *The book of Lord Shang*. London: Probsthain.

Garon, Sheldon. 2011. *Beyond our means: Why America spends while the world saves*. Princeton: Princeton University Press.

Gerschenkron, Alexander. 1962. *Economic backwardness in historical perspective: a book of essays*. Cambridge, MA: Belknap Press of Harvard University Press

Huang, Yiping, and Bijun Wang. 2010. "Cost distortions and structural imbalances in China." *China & World Economy* 18 (4): 1–17.

Kahn, Herman. 1979. *World economic development 1979 and beyond*. Boulder: Westview Press.

Koopmans, Tjalling C. 1969. "Objectives, constraints, and outcomes in optimal growth models." In *Economic models, estimation and risk programming: essays in honor of Gerhard Tintner*, 110–132. Heidelberg: Springer.

Krugman, Paul. 1994. "The myth of Asia's miracle." *Foreign Affairs*: 62–78.

Lazear, Edward P. 2000. "Performance pay and productivity." *American Economic Review* 90 (5): 1346–1361.

Li, Hongbin, Pak Wai Liu, Junsen Zhang, and Ning Ma. 2007. "Economic returns to communist party membership: evidence from urban Chinese twins." *The Economic Journal* 117 (523): 1504–1520.

Li, Hongbin, and Li-An Zhou. 2005. "Political turnover and economic performance: the incentive role of personnel control in China." *Journal of Public Economics* 89 (9–10): 1743–1762.

Lin, Justin Yifu. 2012. *New structural economics: A framework for rethinking development and policy*. Washington: The World Bank.

Ma, Qing-Ping. 2017. "Contribution of interest rate control to China's economic development." *Journal of Chinese Economic and Business Studies* 15 (4): 325–352.

Modigliani, Franco, and Shi Larry Cao. 2004. "The Chinese saving puzzle and the life-cycle hypothesis." *Journal of Economic Literature* 42 (1): 145–170.

North, Douglass Cecil. 1992. *Transaction costs, institutions, and economic performance*. San Francisco, CA: ICS Press

Nove, Alec. 1961. *The soviet economy*. New York: Frederick Praeger.

O'Brien, Kevin J., and Yanhua Deng. 2015. "The reach of the state: work units, family ties and 'harmonious demolition'." *The China Journal* (74): 1–17.

Pierson, Paul. 2000. "Increasing returns, path dependence, and the study of politics." *American Political Science Review* 94 (2): 251–267.

Qiao, Long. 2019. "Official media: stabilization funds doubled over five years, nearly CNY 1.4 trillion." *Radio Free Asia*. Accessed 30 July 2019. rfa.org/mandarin/yataibaodao/zhengzhi/ql1–03142019093727.html.

Ramsey, Frank Plumpton. 1928. "A mathematical theory of saving." *Economic Journal* 38 (152): 543–559.

Shun, Kwong-loi. 1997. *Mencius and early Chinese thought*. Stanford: Stanford University Press.

Solow, Robert M. 1956. "A contribution to the theory of economic growth." *The Quarterly Journal of Economics* 70 (1): 65–94.

Swan, Trevor W. 1956. "Economic growth and capital accumulation." *Economic Record* 32 (2): 334–361.

Waley, Arthur. 2005. *Three ways of thought in ancient China.* Hove, East Sussex: Psychology Press.

Waley, Arthur. 2012. *The analects of Confucius.* London and New York: Routledge.

Wang, Haokai, and Ce Lin. 2014. "Solutions to the predicament of maintaining stability in China." *Investment and Cooperation* (9): 105.

Zhang, Li. 2004. "Forced from home: property rights, civic activism, and the politics of relocation in China." *Urban Anthropology and Studies of Cultural Systems and World Economic Development*: 247–281.

Zhou, Li-An. 2007. "Governing China's local officials: an analysis of promotion tournament model [J]." *Economic Research Journal* 7: 36–50.

4 The future of the China Model

In the preceding chapters we have shown that setting rapid GDP growth as the country's social objective is one of the most important causes of China's phenomenal economic growth. To achieve this rapid growth objective, the government has tried and implemented various measures to maintain high national saving rates and social stability. The institutional arrangements, the historical status of the CPC and the ideological and cultural traditions together have made it possible to have low transaction costs and high saving rates as well as considerable social stability for over four decades (or nearly seven decades if counted from the establishment of the PRC). Because of China's economic success, its current leadership has deviated from the tactics of hiding China's light which was practiced by Deng Xiaoping and Jiang Zemin, and become more assertive, more active and more vocal on the world stage. Many economists inside and outside China, mostly Chinese economists, espouse the China Model of economic development and try to disseminate the message to other developing countries. In this chapter, we will address the following issues: 1) whether other developing countries can adopt the China Model and achieve sustained rapid growth like China's; 2) whether the policies and factors that have enabled China's rapid growth so far can sustain its future growth at a fast pace; and 3) what China should do in future if the policies that have worked very effectively so far become ineffective in promoting economic growth.

4.1 Can other developing countries adopt the China Model successfully?

The supporters of the China Model or the Beijing Consensus think that China has found a new model for developing countries to achieve economic stability and rapid development (Ramo 2004; Zhang 2006). Since the main factor that underlies China's rapid growth is the capacity of the government to maintain a high saving rate and relentlessly cut transaction costs for businesses (which often need to have government connections) while maintaining social stability, if a developing country does not have such a capacity, it may not be able to adopt the China Model. The government's capacity to achieve high saving rates, cut transaction costs and maintain social stability in China arose with the ability of the CPC to control almost all aspects of the society through government offices, mass organizations, public media, information and telecommunications, financial institutions and SOEs. Most governments in developing countries do not have this capacity, therefore, they will not be able to have a saving rate comparable to China's. Without a comparable high saving rate, even if they are at the same level of development as China in 1978, they will not grow as fast as China.

High saving rates usually mean that a higher proportion of national income goes to the wealthy or the state, which is likely to cause social instability in the long run. The current generation would like to have more consumption than leave all the dividends of economic growth to the future generations. In a democracy, economic growth will soon lead to demands for high social welfare, labour protection and increased wages; politicians supporting them will be in power. Therefore it is unlikely that a developing democracy could achieve China's high saving rate and high growth rate. In an authoritarian developing country, if the government controls only the government offices, military and law enforcement, a prolonged extreme pro-business policy is likely to cause political upheavals as the country gets richer. Then the government has to moderate its pro-business policy to the level which can be tolerated by the ordinary people, leading to slower growth.

The combination of authoritarian government and Confucian culture which respects authority and emphasizes hard work provided the social and political conditions for prolonged rapid economic growth. East Asian economies such as South Korea, Taiwan, Singapore and Japan have demonstrated rapid growth under an active government and Confucian culture. Countries with cultural traditions of equality, civil rights and confrontation with authorities would require more consultation and bargaining for governments to carry out development projects, especially when such projects are viewed to benefit big businesses at the expense of the ordinary people or damage the local environment. Generally speaking, in terms of the capacity to maintain both high saving rates and social stability, the governments of most countries do not have a capacity comparable with that of China's government under the leadership of the CPC.

The Chinese culture of hard work and thrift, in addition to the monetary and financial policies of the government, contributes to China's high saving rates. This culture has its root in China's natural environment and history, because often ordinary people have to work hard, to save for difficult times and to be enterprising in order to survive. Countries with natural habitats where foods are more readily available might be less enterprising. Chinese culture promotes strong family bonds and parents save their money for children's education and wellbeing. Since the early 2000s, many parents have to help their children buy an apartment, which is one of the important causes underlying the high demand for residential buildings and the sky rocketing house prices. There is a famous saying about "six purses" available for a young person to buy a new apartment, which means that he can expect financial help from his parents, his mother's parents and his father's parents (Cao 2018). The housing industry has been an important pillar in supporting China's rapid growth in the past 18 years. Without financial support from parents, it probably would not have grown so strongly. East Asian countries historically under Confucian influence tend to have higher saving rates than countries in other regions. It might be difficult for countries with a culture emphasizing current enjoyment and individualism to achieve an economic growth rate comparable to those of China, the four Asian tigers and Japan in the long run.

Although China's rapid growth for four decades is unlikely to be replicated by other developing countries for reasons we have discussed so far, its experiences still provide some useful insights. Firstly, when social stability can be maintained, setting maximum sustainable GDP growth as the social objective promotes economic growth more than setting maximum expected utilitarian social welfare function (SWF)[1] or Rawlsian SWF[2] as the objective. Secondly, markets will guide entrepreneurs to the most profitable industrial sectors appropriate to their resource endowments; entrepreneurs are more dexterous than central planners in identifying where investment should go. Thirdly, tariffs, non-tariff barriers and tax rebates for exports can promote economic growth especially the development of new industrial sectors. Fourthly, pro-business policies at the expense of ordinary citizens facilitate economic growth, but they often accompany corruptions and rent-seeking behaviours of government officials and may eventually lead to social instability.

4.2   Will China sustain its rapid economic growth?

In the past nine years between 2010 and 2018, China's growth rate has dropped from 10.64% to 6.6% according to official statistics. Some scholars think that the actual rate could be substantially lower. For most developed countries and even for many developing countries, 6.6% would be a fairly rapid growth. If we apply the Solow-Swan model to analyze China's growth, the gradual slowdown is an inevitable outcome as China catches up with the developed countries. The smaller the gap between China and the most developed countries, the smaller the difference between China's growth rate and the most developed countries'. The current question facing China's leadership is probably not whether China could regain over 9% average growth rate; rather, it is whether the current around 6.5% growth rate can be sustained for a relatively long period.

4.2.1   Backwardness, catch-up and China's growth rate

An important factor underlying China's rapid growth is its low starting level. Its backwardness gives its catch-up growth more momentum, which results in high growth rates. The Soviet Union had been one of the fastest growing economies between 1920 and 1978 with GDP per capita (PPP) at US$14,099 in 1978, whereas Russia's was US$19,098. In contrast, China's GDP per capita (PPP) is US$1392 in 1978, which is similar to that of the Soviet Union in 1920, and US$12,569 in 2016. Although China has grown much faster than Russia since 1978, whether it will continue to grow faster after its GDP per capita (PPP) exceeds US$19,098 is not certain. Comparing the growth data of some Asian, European and North American economies (Figure 4.1) with their GDP data (Figure 4.2), we can estimate what might happen with China in the future. Between 1950 and 1978, Japan had

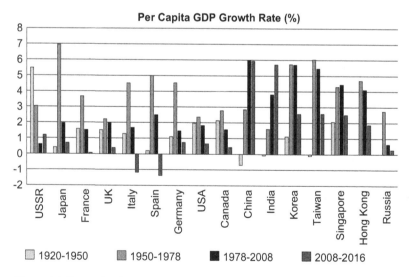

Figure 4.1 Per capita GDP (in 2011 constant international dollars) growth rates of some Asian, European and North American economies

Source: Computed based on Maddison's database (Bolt et al. 2018). There are no 1920–1950 data for Hong Kong and Russia.

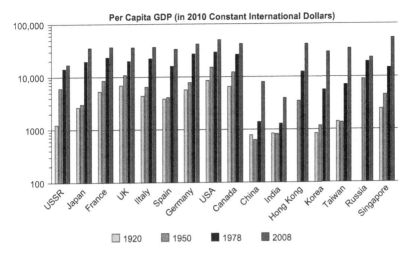

Figure 4.2 Per capita GDP (in 2011 constant international dollars) of some Asian, European and North American economies

Source: According to Maddison's database (Bolt et al. 2018). There are no data for Hong Kong and Russia in 1920.

the highest growth rate with GDP per capita (PPP) being US$19,804 in 1978 and almost caught up with other G7 countries,[3] but its growth rate between 1978 and 2008 is similar to them. The four Asian tigers had 4–6% growth rates between 1950 and 2008, which dropped to around 2.5% (and Hong Kong's dropped to 1.8%) between 2008 and 2016 after surpassing US$30,000 in GDP per capita (PPP). The better performance of the Asian tigers than G7 countries and Spain during 2008–2016 may be attributed to their lower social welfare burden and lower transaction costs.

From the above analysis, it seems that China's economy will continue to grow at a fast pace, but its growth rate will slow down substantially as it approaches US$20,000. Russia and the former Soviet Union started to stagnate after reaching US$19,098 and US$14,099, respectively, whereas G7 countries and the four Asian tigers still have moderate to fairly high growth rates after reaching US$20,000. One explanation might be that central planning is effective in catching up from a low-level GDP per capita during the paradigm-changing growth because of its capacity to raise national saving rates. Once the paradigm change which relies on high investment has completed, the ensuing normal growth depends more on small incremental innovations which are hindered by the rigidity and conservatism of the central planning system. China's rapid growth depends not only on the deregulation and marketization, but also on the advantage of backwardness. Given the rapid growth of the Soviet Union between 1920 and 1978 with an average annual rate 4.29% (compared with the second fastest Japan's 3.52%), China might still have achieved growth rates comparable with its current ones, had it continued to use the central planning system.

The rapid economic growth of the Soviet Union, the Asian tigers and China share the common feature of high saving rates and low consumption rates, which implies a larger share of national income going to capital (owners) and a smaller share to labour. The high saving rate means that the increased output cannot be consumed domestically and it has to be cleared to avoid overproduction-caused economic crisis. For the Asian tigers, Japan and China adopting the export-led growth model, the surplus output was mainly consumer goods and export to more developed countries. For the Soviet Union, the increased production capacity was used to produce investment goods and military equipment, so instead of oversupply there was actually a shortage of consumer goods relative to the increased income following rapid economic growth.

Huge investment in the heavy industry produced more investment goods and eventually led the heavy industry to its own steady state, at which more investment can no longer lead to more growth. Economic stagnation, shortage of consumer goods compared with Western countries and bureaucratic indifference toward the complaints of ordinary people exacerbated discontent of the population, forcing the Soviet leadership to consider reforming the system. The introduction of market mechanism caused 1) huge losses and bankruptcy of heavy industry firms whose products have little market demand except fulfilling centrally planned targets, and 2) price hikes of consumer goods in short supply. Both effects will decrease the living standard of ordinary people. In contrast, countries with export-led growth model could adapt to the slowdown of export growth more smoothly by increasing the income and welfare of ordinary people.

4.2.2   Will China's exports continue to lead rapid economic growth?

Exports will have a much smaller role in driving China's economic growth in the future, because export growth cannot be faster than the GDP growth rate of the importing countries in the long run. When China's exports gradually take over the market of manufactured goods in developed countries due to the competitiveness of goods made in China, its export growth can be much faster than the GDP growth rate of developed countries. The faster export growth accompanies the shrinking of the same sectors of the importing countries. When commodity markets in developed countries have been saturated by goods made in China, its exports would no longer be able to grow faster than the GDP growth rate of developed countries. If China's export sector grows at the GDP growth rate of the importing countries, for example, 2–3%, it can only help to drive China's economy for 2–3% growth. China's export growth rate has dropped to the level of its own GDP growth rate since 2012. Although China tries to expand exports to developing countries through the Belt and Road Initiatives, we can expect further decrease in its export growth rate.

The thriving housing industry and the massive investment in infrastructure in the past 18 years have reduced the relative weight of exports in China's GDP and the impact of exports on GDP growth. China's early growth after 1978 depended on the same export-led growth model as Japan, South Korea, Taiwan, Hong Kong and Singapore in their early growth stage. At the beginning of China's reform and opening, its economy was much smaller and a sizable increase in the total net export would result in a substantial percentage increase in the GDP. The foreign trade multiplier[4] further enhanced the impact of export on the GDP growth. As the economy becomes larger and larger, especially with massive domestic investment in infrastructure such as motorways, high-speed railways, airports, ports, bridges and telecommunications, the export growth in recent years has a much smaller contribution to the GDP growth than before the 2007–2008 financial crisis. Between 2004 and 2008, China's exports-to-GDP ratio was over 30% and the export growth rate was around 25%. The ratio has dropped to below 20% since 2016.

The growth in China's GDP per capita will increase its labour costs and slow export growth. As labour costs in China increase, its comparative advantage in labour-intensive industries gradually disappears. Other developing countries such as those in Southeast and South Asian countries like Vietnam become more competitive and start to take market shares from China, which will also reduce the contribution of exports to China's economic growth. China's strategy to deal with the loss of competitiveness in labour-intensive products is to move up the product ladder and to develop technology-intensive sectors. The Made in China 2025 plan reflects this strategy. China intends to become a world leader in advanced manufacturing by providing government support, subsidies and trade protection to Chinese high-tech firms (Kennedy 2015).

China's strategy to become a major player in technology-intensive sectors has caused concern in Western countries that their remaining industrial territories would be taken by China's SOEs with state subsidies. When China's economy was small and exports were mainly labour-intensive products, developed countries were more tolerant to China's protectionist measures on its industrial sectors. This tolerance is guided by the theory of comparative advantage in international trade. Economists believe that countries would all have their maximum benefits if they specialize in producing the goods for which they have comparative advantage. So China can specialize in producing goods for which developed countries do not have the comparative advantage. This was considered as international division of labour (Baek 2005). As China's economy grows and its enterprises enter the high-tech sectors and compete with firms in developed countries, developed countries become increasingly wary of China's trade barrier and state subsidies to high-tech industries which they think give Chinese firms unfair advantages over foreign firms.

The trade war waged by US President Donald Trump is to defend the remaining industrial territory where the US still has absolute as well as comparative advantage. Paul Samuelson shows that the theory of comparative advantage breaks down when a country (China) has improved its productivity in producing the goods for which it did not have comparative advantage, and the more developed country (the US) will be worse off compared with the previous equilibrium (Samuelson 2004). Although China's leaders enthusiastically preach free trade, vow to defend free trade at various international forums and accuse the US of protectionism, China has much more protectionist measures and practices than the US and other developed countries for justifiable or unjustifiable reasons. At the beginning of China's reform and opening, China did need protectionist measures to protect its infant industries and developed countries acquiesced in those measures.

Since China has become the factory of the world, the US has become less tolerant to China's protectionist practices. The Trump administration tries to use punitive tariffs to press China to open its markets and reduce state subsidies to China's SOEs, so that foreign and Chinese firms have a level playing field. On 6 July 2018, the Trump administration imposed a 25% tariff on 818 categories of goods imported from China worth of US$50 billion, and China retaliated with tariffs on goods from the US worth of US$34 billion. On 24 September 2018, the US imposed a 10% tariff against China's exports valued at over US$200 billion (Tankersley and Bradsher 2018) which was raised to 25% on 10 May 2019, and China retaliated with tariffs on US$60 billion of US exports to China. On 1 August 2019 US President Trump announced imposition of 10% tariffs on the remaining US$300 billion imports from China from 1 September 2019. On 24 August 2019 he announced imposition of additional 5% tariffs on all US$550 billion worth of goods imports from China in response to China's retaliation of 5–10% additional tariffs on US$75 billion worth of imports from the US. The trade war will also reduce the contribution of exports to China's economic growth.

4.2.3 Will China's domestic demand sustain rapid economic growth?

Since China's exports can no longer drive China's rapid growth, it needs to increase its domestic demand. China's domestic demand includes consumption, investment and government expenditure. Investment has been one of the key drivers for economic growth in China, both in the expansion of the export sector and in the construction of infrastructure and residential buildings. However, the Solow-Swan model has indicated that high investment rates cannot lead to fast growth once the economy reaches its steady state. For example, Singapore still has 40–50% national saving rates during 2008–2016 (Figure 4.3), but its growth rate of per capita GDP (PPP) has dropped to around 2.5% (Figure 4.1). India's saving rate is over 10 percentage points lower than Singapore's, but its growth rate is 5.71% during 2008–2016. Therefore, high saving rates cannot ensure China's rapid growth in future. Moreover, the low interest rate policy has induced overinvestment to the extent that almost all industrial sectors, where entry is not controlled by the government, have huge overcapacity (Shen and Chen 2017). The government has to enforce production capacity reduction in many sectors by administrative orders. Local governments at the municipal level are heavily in debts through the nominally independent infrastructure investment platforms, which borrowed heavily from banks and invested for infrastructure construction (Pan et al. 2017). The overcapacity of all sectors and heavy indebtedness of local governments make it inefficient and infeasible to use investment to maintain the momentum of China's rapid growth. The

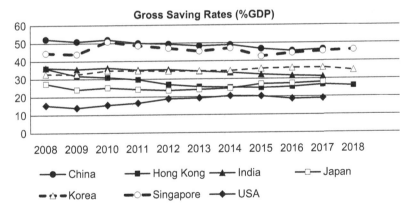

Figure 4.3 Gross saving rates of Mainland China, Hong Kong, India, Japan, Korea, Singapore and US during 2008–2018

Source: World Bank.

advanced manufacturing has been planned as the area for more investment, but state subsidies involved in the Made in China 2025 plan have been one of the hot issues in the Sino–US trade disputes.

China's policy-makers appear to tread very cautiously in building China's social security system and the government will not sharply increase welfare spending in near future, so increasing consumption is the main approach for enhancing domestic demand. China's government and policy-makers fully understand that increasing consumption demand is the right approach for maintaining China's growth momentum. However, although the uneven wealth distribution in China helps its investment growth because rich people spend a small proportion of their income on consumption, it does not help the growth of domestic consumption. China's Gini index is around 0.48 according to the National Bureau of Statistics of China, which is higher than most developed countries (Molero-Simarro 2017). During the early growth stage of developing countries, it is usually the case that income and wealth are more concentrated to a small percentage of the population. The successful entrepreneurs and senior managers tend to get a larger share than the labourers, because capital stock and technologies are rare resources and labour is more abundant. The income inequality with a large proportion of low-income people is the main obstacle for China to increase its domestic consumption demand. The low-level social welfare benefits and high housing prices also inhibit the growth of China's domestic consumption.

Low social welfare benefits force residents to save for health care, children's education and post-retirement living, while high housing prices reduce the disposable income of ordinary households for consumption. To increase domestic consumption demand, usually the best way is to increase the wages of low-income workers. However, increasing wages will increase labour costs and decrease the international competitiveness of Chinese products. The private enterprises now provide over 80% employment, but many firms find it difficult to carry on their business in recent years. Private enterprises have to bear high non-wage employment costs and other costs in highly competitive markets, so it seems unlikely for private firms to substantially increase wages of low-income workers. Since the potential of deregulation in the competitive sectors has been fully realized, now it is the time to open up the remaining monopolistic sectors, but the government is reluctant to open up the monopolized sectors in which almost only SOEs are allowed to operate.

The housing industry has been a key component of investment and contributed substantially to the rapid economic growth since 2004, but the high housing prices have hindered the domestic consumption growth (Chamon and Prasad 2010). The housing industry might not contribute significantly to the economic growth in future, because the high price will start to discourage demand sometime in future. More importantly, as China's population is expected to decrease due to the one-child policy implemented over 30 years (Croll, Davin, and Kane 2013), there will be an oversupply of secondhand apartments when the parents of the first "sole child" generation become unable to live independently. Besides their own apartment, each first sole child household will inherit two more apartments from their respective parents. The Minsky moment of China's housing market will come eventually.

A decreasing and aging population will decrease domestic consumption growth. China's one-child policy might have produced substantial demographic dividends in its early stage of growth after its reform and opening, but the dividends will turn negative when the sole child generation becomes the major part of the workforce (Croll, Davin, and Kane 2013). As China's population aging proceeds much faster than developed countries, China might face labour shortage if artificial intelligence and robotics do not mature fast enough to supplement or replace human workers. Since retired people tend to have much lower demand for high-end consumption goods than those for daily care and everyday necessities, population aging and reduced population, especially young population, will slow consumption growth substantially, leading to slower economic growth. The recent emphasis on developing artificial intelligence and robotics by China's leadership might reflect their awareness of China's low birth rate and impending labour shortage.

4.2.4 *Government capacity to govern*

Although the CPC still has full control of the government and most mass organizations, its capacity to govern has been more constrained than in the early days of reform and opening. In the early days, the CPC wielded absolute power and authority over the whole country and people accepted whatever the CPC told them and looked up to the CPC for direction in general. The CPC loosened its ideological control during the 1980s, many Western ideas entered China and people within and outside the CPC started to reflect on what had happened during the Cultural Revolution and since 1949 (Perry 2007). As the truth about China and Western countries was being revealed to ordinary Chinese people, the spiritual authority of the CPC was much reduced. Improvements in the legal system, though far from perfect and often abused, give people more confidence to stand up to the government and also put more constraints on what the government can do to enforce its plans. The self-awareness of ordinary people and legal constraints on the behaviours of the government will slow implementation of government-sponsored or government-supported business development projects, thus decreasing the economic growth rate.

The economic reform produced a thriving private sector and the government no longer controls all food and jobs. The authority of the CPC and its capacity to enforce its plans have been gradually eroded by the rise of the private sector (O'brien 1998). The less reliant on the government for ordinary people to make a living, the more likely they will defend their rights and bargain with the government. The awareness by ordinary people of their constitutional and legal rights will increase transaction costs and reduce the economic growth rate in the short run. Since China's government will have a decreasing capacity to push through development plans and to support enterprises in their transactions with workers and households, the component in China's past growth rate due to the reduction in bargaining time and implementation costs will disappear.

In developed countries, development projects need time-consuming consultation processes with relevant parties. If a certain party feels that its interest has been infringed by a development project, it may challenge the government decision at a court. These could significantly delay the completion of a development project, but it has the advantage to reach a Pareto optimal solution in which every party feels that its utility has not been reduced. The reduced government authority in accelerating business development projects by cutting bargaining time and purchasing costs for enterprises will slow China's economic growth, but it will lead to more Pareto-improving outcomes from business transactions in China.

4.3   What should China do to sustain rapid economic growth?

China's recent growth rate has been around 6.5%, and some scholars think that the actual rate could be much lower. According to the Solow-Swan model, without technological progress, the per capita output will stop growing when an economy has reached its steady state. The factors that underlie China's rapid growth so far will eventually become insufficient to sustain China's rapid growth. However, the huge difference between China and the US in income per capita indicates that there is still a huge growth potential for China, even if we take into account the strength of the US in its natural environment, per capita resources and the special status of US dollars in the global monetary system. Can China tap into this growth potential and sustain its growth rate at the current level for many years to come? This depends on whether China can adequately address the structural issues in its economy, manage the real estate bubble, improve its social security system, reduce income inequality, become more open in international economic relations and promote rule of law.

4.3.1   *Address structural issues*

The current makeup of China's economy has served China's growth well so far. China's government allowed private enterprises to operate during the 1980s and sold all the small and most medium-sized SOEs to their managers or other private enterprises in the late 1990s, which solved motivation and incentive problems and greatly stimulated China's economic growth. Now the thriving private sector contributes 50% of the GDP, 60% of the tax revenues and 80% of the urban employment. The provinces with the highest four GDPs per capita, Zhejiang, Jiangsu, Fujian and Guangdong, all have a thriving private sector and their employees of state owned units (SOUs, including SOEs and government offices) are 15%, 14%, 19% and 17% of the total employment, respectively. Beijing and Shanghai, the two municipalities which have the top two GDPs per capita among the 31 provincial level divisions in the mainland, have many SOE headquarters and government offices, but their SOU employees are still only 20% of the total employment (National Bureau of Statistics of China). Therefore, provinces with an active and large private sector are more likely to be prosperous (Tian 2001). Since the deregulated industries have almost reached their full potential in driving China's rapid growth, the currently monopolized industries need to be opened for competition, which will provide new impetus to China's economic growth.

Many of the SOEs especially the so-called central enterprises operate in monopolized industries or sectors which have administrative barriers for entry such as electricity, petroleum, natural gas, railway, civil aviation, telecommunications and defence industry. The monopolized industries employed less than 8% of workers, but their employees used to earn more than 55% of total wage and non-wage incomes of all employees in China. The employees of the SOEs have a much higher average income than that of private firms, while the return on capital of SOEs is generally much lower than that of private firms. The SOEs hold around 65% of the total assets and receive two-thirds of the bank loans, but they only contribute less than one-third of the total tax revenues and 20% of the urban employment. In the 40 industry categories where both private firms and SOEs operate, the return on capital of private firms is far higher than that of SOEs in 34 sectors. One approach to promote economic growth at the present is to reduce monopoly and open up monopolized industries to private capital, but this seems to conflict with one of Deng Xiaoping's Four Adherences, adherence to the socialist road.

China's tax system should increase the weight of direct taxes and reduce the proportion of indirect taxes to stimulate consumption growth. The dominance of indirect taxes in China's tax income has increased the price level and decreased domestic consumption; hence, low-income households bear a higher proportion of tax burden than high income households. Although it benefits the capital owners and entrepreneurs and promotes economic growth because rich people save a higher proportion of their incomes, it inhibits the growth of domestic consumption which becomes more and more important for China's future growth. Moreover, concentrating wealth in the hand of rich people does not help maintain social stability and sustain economic growth in the long run.

4.3.2   Manage the real estate bubble

China's housing market has been a key contributor to China's economic growth in the past 18 years, but high housing prices have also increased production costs and diverted resources from manufacturing to real estate investment. Since house prices have increased at a pace much faster than GDP growth, many Chinese people deeply believe that house prices will never decrease. China's central and local governments have intervened to prop up prices each time house prices show signs of decline. The belief of continually increasing house prices reinforces itself as Chinese households which have invested their wealth in real estate make spectacular returns (Glaeser et al. 2017). However, this trend of increasing prices may not continue because of demographic changes. The urban family structure in China now becomes 4:2:1 or 4:2:2, that is, four grandparents, the father and the mother, and one or two children. If the grandparents and the parents all have their own apartments, the only child will have three apartments to inherit. If he or she is to marry another child of the same situation, the married couple will have six apartments. As the population ages and decreases, an eventual burst of the property bubble is unavoidable. The government needs to manage it well, because a large sum of wealth has been invested in housing properties since 2002. A sudden burst of the bubble at some future date might severely dent the confidence of businesspeople as well as ordinary households.

The following measures might be considered to manage the burst of a property bubble. Firstly, the government should have a transparent plan to assess and manage the property bubble. So far governments at all levels seem to be happy with high house prices, which bring more land income to the government and pull the demand for many other industries. Clear information on housing per se might cause the collapse of the housing market, but blindly inflating the property bubble would be worse. Secondly, as land is a scarce resource in China and occupancy of more land should be discouraged, property tax should be imposed to save land. Property tax should be implemented with sufficient transition time to smooth the process. Thirdly, education, health and cultural resources should be more widely distributed across the country. Currently these resources are too concentrated in a few megacities. With more resources and more opportunities in medium and small cities, the house prices in megacities are likely to drop.

4.3.3 Improve social security system and reduce income inequality

With uncertainties in life, most people tend to save more than they actually need because of risk aversion. Over-saving is conducive to economic growth when capital is scarce and production capacity is overutilized. However, when overcapacity is the main issue and domestic demand is insufficient for sustaining rapid economic growth, over-saving becomes a hindrance to economic growth. China's high saving rate is mainly due to savings of SOEs and private enterprises, but household savings also contribute to a substantial part. An improved social security system where healthcare costs above a certain level are provided by the state will reduce household saving and stimulate economic growth.

A more important part of the national savings is those held by SOEs and private enterprises. Opening up the monopolized sectors and letting in the competition will decrease prices of their products and services, increase consumer surplus and reduce income inequality among individuals. For the time being, private investments are all in those competitive sectors and the resources are not optimally allocated across all sectors. If the monopolized industries are open to private investment, the optimal resource allocation between previously monopolized sectors and other sectors will close their wage gap. To reduce the national savings from the SOEs, the government should transfer more money from the profits of the SOEs to social security funds. Income inequality is a key factor in causing slow growth in domestic consumption. Improving social security system will not only increase domestic consumption, but also help maintain social stability.

4.3.4 Become more open in international relations

China had more than its fair share of hardship, misery and humiliations in its modern history especially in dealing with Western powers, so that many Chinese, especially the CPC, have a profound distrust of foreign countries. China's leadership and many Chinese people view Western countries as rivals who want to prevent China from regaining its past glory rather than partners in economic affairs. Because Western media are largely blocked by China's government, many ordinary Chinese people believe in what the government said and become indignant on requests from foreign countries. During the reform and opening, China has implemented more protection measures for its infant industries than Western countries. As China has become the factory of the world, it can afford to let Chinese firms compete with foreign firms at a level playing field.

China's government and people prefer firms and resources to be controlled by Chinese. They are proud of successes achieved by Chinese firms and give many helps to facilitate their success. China's government may need to consider more of the interests of ordinary Chinese people rather than the interests of big companies when making policy decisions. There is no need at the present time to give special benefits to foreign firms investing in China, neither is there special need to favour firms who brand themselves Chinese but have registered in foreign countries and whose majority shareholders are foreigners. No matter whether the owners are Chinese or not, as long as they provide better services to Chinese people, the government should provide them the same convenience as Chinese-owned firms.

4.3.5   Promote the rule of law

Why do rich Chinese people including many senior government and CPC officials send their children abroad to study and transfer their personal wealth abroad? Some have done so because their wealth were obtained illegally in China so that they want to avoid punishment. Others might have done so because they fear the uncertainty of China's legal system. Therefore, the CPC and the government should promote the rule of law. When the rule of law is upheld, there will be fewer corrupt officials and less illegally obtained wealth, and rich successful businesspeople will sleep well in the night. Promoting the rule of law will increase the time costs of transaction and the monetary costs of business, but it will reduce wealth and income inequality and increase the overall utility of Chinese people. At the current level of GDP, letting businesspeople take a larger share of output to stimulate investment is no longer conducive to economic growth, so it is time to let ordinary people get what they should have through negotiation and bargaining to achieve Pareto optimal distribution of incomes.

With the rule of law and a government of service providers rather than decision-making patriarchs, new technologies will thrive. The reason is simple, the people who know best of future technologies are those who are researching on them, it is better to let venture capitalists to finance them. The decisions by government officials to choose the eventual winner are more likely to be wrong and crowding out the true innovators, the same phenomenon as bad money drives out good. The rule of law economically helps achieve Pareto-optimal solutions, and politically contributes to the social stability which Chinese people had strived for 100 years before the establishment of the People's Republic of China.

4.4   Summary

China's high saving rates, low transaction costs and high transaction efficiency underlie China's rapid economic growth. China's institutions, especially the leadership of the CPC and its pro-business policies since 1978, have ensured high saving rates as well as social stability. If other developing countries do not have the institutions to ensure high saving rates and social stability, they cannot replicate China's success.

China's growth has followed the technological path explored by developed countries and East Asian newly industrialized economies. High saving rates will lead to high growth rates, but as China's output level approaches the steady state determined by the current technology, its growth will inevitably slow down even with high saving rates. Overinvestment will reduce return on capital such that investment becomes ineffective in promoting growth. Exports cannot grow faster than the GDP growth rate of the importing countries after their market has been saturated by Chinese products. High saving rates and income inequality hinder domestic consumption growth. Improvements in the legal system and more people with high education and culture level put more constraints on government capacity to enforce development projects. These will all contribute to the slowdown of China's economic growth.

Although the slowdown is inevitable, opening monopolized sectors for competition, improving social security system, reducing income inequality, facilitating international trade and promoting the rule of law will help maintain the current growth rate for a longer period. These measures will also increase the utility of the current population as well as the total utility of all generations, reduce the probability of social upheavals due to income inequality and improve international relations.

Notes

1 The utilitarian social welfare function (SWF) measures a society's welfare by adding all individual utility values. For comparison between societies with different populations, the average-utilitarian SWF is usually used and the average utility is the total utility divided by the number of individuals.
2 The Rawlsian SWF measures a society's welfare as the utility of the individual who is worst off.
3 G7 countries include Canada, France, Germany, Italy, Japan, the UK and the US.
4 Foreign trade multiplier (also called export multiplier) is the amount of the national income raised by a unit increase in domestic investment on exports.

References

Baek, Seung-Wook. 2005. "Does China follow 'the East Asian development model'?" *Journal of Contemporary Asia* 35 (4): 485–498.

Bolt, Jutta, Robert Inklaar, Herman de Jong, and Jan Luiten van Zanden. 2018. *Maddison Project database*. www.ggdc.net/maddison.

Cao, Qi. 2018. "Five wealth management proposals to young people." *Farmers Get Rich* (11): 62.

Chamon, Marcos D., and Eswar S. Prasad. 2010. "Why are saving rates of urban households in China rising?" *American Economic Journal: Macroeconomics* 2 (1): 93–130.

Croll, Elisabeth, Delia Davin, and Penny Kane. 2013. "China's one-child family policy." *British Medical Journal* 19 (4): 39–63.

Glaeser, Edward, Wei Huang, Yueran Ma, and Andrei Shleifer. 2017. "A real estate boom with Chinese characteristics." *Journal of Economic Perspectives* 31 (1): 93–116.

Kennedy, Scott. 2015. "Made in China 2025." *Center for Strategic and international Studies*. Last Modified 1 June 2015. Accessed 30 July 2019. www.csis.org/analysis/made-china-2025.

Molero-Simarro, Ricardo. 2017. "Inequality in China revisited. The effect of functional distribution of income on urban top incomes, the urban-rural gap and the Gini index, 1978–2015." *China Economic Review* 42: 101–117.

O'Brien, Maire. 1998. "Dissent and the emergence of civil society in post-totalitarian China." *Journal of Contemporary China* 7 (17): 153–166.

Pan, Fenghua, Fengmei Zhang, Shengjun Zhu, and Dariusz Wójcik. 2017. "Developing by borrowing? Inter-jurisdictional competition, land finance and local debt accumulation in China." *Urban Studies* 54 (4): 897–916.

Perry, Elizabeth J. 2007. "Studying Chinese politics: farewell to revolution?" *China Journal* 57 (57): 1–22.

Ramo, Joshua Cooper. 2004. *The Beijing consensus*. London: Foreign Policy Centre

Samuelson, Paul A. 2004. "Where Ricardo and Mill rebut and confirm arguments of mainstream economists supporting globalization." *Journal of Economic Perspectives* 18 (3): 135–146.

Shen, Guangjun, and Binkai Chen. 2017. "Zombie firms and over-capacity in Chinese manufacturing." *China Economic Review* 44: 327–342.

Tankersley, Jim, and Keith Bradsher. 2018. "Trump hits China with tariffs on $200 billion in goods, escalating trade war." *New York Times*, 17 September 2018.

Tian, Xiaowen. 2001. "Privatization and economic performance: evidence from Chinese provinces." *Economic Systems* 25 (1): 65–77.

Zhang, Weiwei. 2006. "The allure of the Chinese model." *International Herald Tribune*, 2 November 2006.

Index

Printed in the United States
by Baker & Taylor Publisher Services